D1104909

A
Christian Response
to the
HOLOCAUST

by
Harry James Cargas

Foreword by
Elie Wiesel

Stonehenge
books

1582 S. Parker Road
Denver, Colorado 80231

3/24/73 $

To Express My Gratitude

It hardly suffices to put a few words on paper as a form of gratitude for ongoing assistance given me by a number of people. Yet how else . . . ?

Adam and Judy Aronson, my friends, have been so supportive, in so many ways, and for so extended a period, that truly without their help this book, and much else that I write, would never have been completed.

While doing research at Yad Vashem Holocaust Memorial Center in Jerusalem, I was enthusiastically assisted by Chana Abells and knowledgeably guided by one of the world's great Holocaust scholars, Dr. Livia Rothkirchen.

My friend, Rabbi Sol Bernards, of the Anti-Defamation League in New York City, has been a source of understanding and inspiration to me in my work.

Once again the assistance of Maureen O'Brien Thielemeier and Margret Brown in preparing a manuscript for me have proven wonderfully helpful.

Grants from two organizations freed me for the months necessary to organize and write much that is in this book. One was awarded me be the Shlomo Zalman and Shoshana Strochlitz Foundation of New London, Connecticut, and I am particularly grateful to Mr. Sigmund Strochlitz and Romana R. Primus, M.D., for their aid on my behalf.

The second was a grant from the Monsanto Fund. I am indebted especially to its Director, Mr. William Symes, for his interest in my work.

Finally, I must say that whatever is of merit in my work on the Holocaust has been profoundly influenced by the writing and friendship of Elie Wiesel. More than anyone, this man continues to be my teacher. No doubt I have not learned enough; I shall continue to strive. My obligations to Wiesel are great and unrepayable. He knows that I shall attempt to fulfill them, nevertheless.

I have learned from Jews and Christians as I pursued my research in Holocaust studies. My gratitude for their work, their encouragement and their friendship cannot be measured. This book is an inadequate indication of my appreciation:

Alice Eckardt
Roy Eckardt
Eva Fleischner
Nora Levin
Franklin Littell
John Pawlikowski
John Roth
Livia Rothkirchen
Elie Wiesel

My photo on the jacket is courtesy of Tom Oates.

Foreword

It has been said often, and it can never be said enough: The Event remains unique, unlike any other. Product of History, it transcends History. The burden of its horror weighing upon all aspects of the human experience, it goes beyond everything. Auschwitz: the ultimate mystery. Impossible to enter it from the outside. Whoever has not lived through it will never know, never understand it. Treblinka: kingdom of another world, symbol of total defeat. There, man finds himself condemned, robbed of all hopes, all illusions.

The few survivors themselves will confirm it: the Event defies all analogy; it can only be compared to itself. It defies understanding as well as language. No one can comprehend or describe it. To explain is to diminish it, to generalize is to mutilate it. The Holocaust demands interrogation and calls everything into question. Traditional ideas and acquired values, philosophical systems and social theories—all must be revised in the shadow of Birkenau. Novelists and politicians, poets and moralists, theologians and scholars— all feel compelled to examine their consciences with regard to the Holocaust. Not to do so would mean to live a lie.

Although essentially Jewish, the Event has universal significance. It calls out to all men, but, of course, in different ways.

We all want to know: how was it possible? The killers killed and the world was silent . . . The killers were able to kill because the world was indifferent. The indifference of those days obliges us to take a stand today.

This is what Harry James Cargas does in his upsetting and disturbing work which will make the reader, whatever his faith, reflect and weep.

A fervent and faithful Christian, the author expresses

his anguish and sadness: it is impossible to detach the Final Solution from its Christian context. The murder of six million Jews is at the same time part of Jewish and Christian history. On all levels, the questions are disturbing. How does one explain that a Hitler or a Himmler were never excommunicated by the Church? that Pope Pius XII never judged it necessary or essential to condemn Auschwitz or Maidanek? that the killers came from Christian families and had received a Christian education? and that many Catholic and Protestant dignitaries had supported the Nazis?

Certainly, here and there, courageous Christians faced danger and came to the aid of the Jews; we shall be eternally grateful to them. But they were few in number. They were the exceptions. As a general rule, the Jewish victims rarely found refuge. In Christian Poland, so hostile was the countryside that those who escaped from the ghettos often returned to them; they feared the Poles as much as the Germans. In Lithuania too. In the Ukraine. In Hungary. And yet in all of these occupied countries, there were resistance movements that had their heroes and martyrs. Only the Jews were victims of the Nazi invaders and of their victims as well.

How is one to understand, to explain, this Christianity bereft of charity and compassion? As a Jew, I have always been reluctant to explore the question. Let us thank Harry James Cargas for having done so. The things he says about his Christian brothers and friends will be painful to them; one hopes they will not turn away. Thanks to this book, they will learn what others have hidden from them for so long: that the love of God is whole only if expressed through the love of man.

Elie Wiesel
Translated from the French by Ellen S. Fine

Introduction

A POST-AUSCHWITZ CATHOLIC

To call myself a Roman Catholic is to describe my spiritual development incompletely. It is more honest for me to say at this time in my life that I am a post-Auschwitz Catholic, in the wider context of Western Christianity. The Holocaust event requires my response precisely as a Christian. The Holocaust is, in my judgment, the greatest tragedy for Christians since the crucifixion. In the first instance, Jesus died; in the latter, Christianity may be said to have died. In the case of Christ, the Christian believes in a resurrection. Will there be, can there be, a resurrection for Christianity? That is the question that obsesses me. Am I a part of a religious body which in fact is a fossil rather than a living entity? Can one be a Christian today, given the death camps which, in major part, were conceived, built and operated by a people who called themselves Christians and some of whom—records prove, their own words prove—took pride in this work?

The failure of Christianity in the mid-20th century is monumental. Is it fatal? I need to know. This seems to me to be the main question facing people who today call themselves Christian.

It is too easy to say of those who lived and persecuted *or remained "neutral"* in Germany, Poland, Russia, Austria, Czechoslovakia, Latvia, Hungary, Bulgaria, Greece, France and other nations during the Nazi era that, although they regarded themselves as Christians, they really weren't. That's too smug an answer. One implication of such a response is that we who now look back and say that "they weren't really Christian" are eager to submit ourselves as authentic Christians. How can we be certain that when the time comes for us to be heroic Christians (in theory, at least, the expression is redundant!) we will not collapse? All women and men are failures at their religion in some degree. But have we Christians, with our history of the persecution of Jews—with the Inquisition, the Crusades, pogroms, anti-Judaism and the Holocaust—established a tradition of failure from which there is no escape?

The reasons for my own personal conversion to Roman Catholicism at age 19 are not important. The act of commitment is decisive, however. I wished to share then, as I do now, in the many and great glories of that institution. I think it proper to say that I was obsessed with becoming as good a Christian as I could. Today it may be more accurate to say that I am obsessed with judging that original obsession. Was it valid or not? Am I a fool to be an active member of a church which proclaims love as its motivating energy when historically . . . ?

I let the question hang. I'm not even sure how to ask it. Others will perhaps rephrase it as they too search. It is one comfort to me that I do know an increasing number of Christians who are engaged in such an investigation. To ask the question by oneself isolates one so greatly that it may be spiritually perilous. Raised in a tradition of fear of an all-powerful God who can punish the blasphemous—and questioning the validity of Christianity will be seen by some as precisely that—the question can be explored only at serious risk to one's spiritual health. However, some reflective Christians are at the point today in their spiritual development that it is blasphemous *not* to raise the question.

Silence, which can be holy, can also be sinful. Silence in the face of the Holocaust, I submit, is truly blasphemy. It is part of Christian teaching that God exists in every person. We dare not forget, then, that 1,000,000 Jewish child-Gods were murdered by the Nazis and their collaborators in World War II. Five million other Jewish-Gods were slaughtered there also. Perhaps another 9,000,000 non-Jewish-Gods were massacred as well.

My obsession with what I call the Christian Holocaust derives from the statistics cited above. Some Jews have been suspicious of my motives—I cannot blame them, given the history of Jewish-Christian encounters. Some Christians have been suspicious of my motives as well. Their suspicions are less understandable.

Through all of this, I have come to the conclusion that Albert Camus was profoundly correct when he said that "on this earth there are pestilences and there are victims, and it's up to us, so far as is possible, not to join forces with the pestilences." And Elie Wiesel was profoundly correct when he wrote that "he who is not among the victims is with the executioners." And Viktor Frankl is profoundly correct when he concludes that "we may learn that there are two races of men in this world, but only these two—the 'race' of the decent man and the 'race' of the indecent man."

Thus I must conclude that to identify myself as a Roman Catholic, in the shadow of recent history, is inaccurate, incomplete, even misleading. Culturally, of course, I am that, but spiritually I put on the mantle of a post-Auschwitz Catholic. It is in this concept that all of my work—indeed my life—is now rooted.

Harry James Cargas

I

CENTURIES OF CHRISTIAN
PERSECUTION OF THE JEWS

The massacre of Jews in the Second World War, and all that accompanied that prolonged, monstrous event, is the greatest Christian tragedy since the crucifixion of Jesus. The Holocaust was the culmination, in great part, of Christian teachings about Jews, of misinterpreted and erroneous theology. After preaching love of others for nearly two thousand years, it was, in the main, people who called themselves Christian who slaughtered women because they were Jewish, who slaughtered men because they were Jewish, who slaughtered babies because they were Jewish.

Jews have asked over and over again, Where was God at Auschwitz?—using the name of the most infamous of the death camps to stand for all of them. Some Jewish people of faith said that the torture and death of 6,000,000 Jews—6,000,000, over one-third of all of the Jews in the world—some said that these deaths, and the sufferings of the comparatively few who survived imprisonment, marked the birth pangs of the coming of the Messiah, that Messiah for whom the Jews have been waiting these many centuries. Other Jews were not so optimistic.'One group, in a death camp, held a trial of God. They found God guilty of breaking the Covenant made with the chosen people and of abandoning them to the horrors of near annihilation.

Adolph Hitler, a baptized Catholic who was never excommunicated by Rome, implemented a policy of total destruction because, and only because, *he was able to.* Only because people willingly cooperated in individual and mass murders. Who, for example, were the architects who designed the ovens into which people were delivered for cremation? Who meticulously executed the plans for the efficient gas chambers into which naked men, women and children were herded to die? Who originated the design for the camps, those models of economical, technological destruction? Which firms bid on the contracts to build the camps, the gas chambers, the ovens? Who bribed whom to win the coveted contracts, to gain the chance to make a profit and serve the Fuehrer by erecting houses of death and torture? Which doctors performed experiments on Jewish victims? Who shaved their heads, and all bodily hairs, to gain materials for cloth and rugs? We've heard of lampshades made from Jewish skins, of soap made from Jewish bodies, of "enforcers" throwing Jewish victims—most of them dead, but not all—into huge pits, of brutal guards crushing Jewish babies' skulls with rifle butts, and shooting aged and unhealthy Jews who couldn't keep up on forced marches, and forcing naked Jews to stand for hours in freezing weather for either convenience or amusement. Who were these tormentors? What of the train engineers who guided the cattle cars packed with starving, dying, dead Jews to their locales of interment? And what of the ordinary citizens of many European nations who, as the death trains passed through their communities, would throw bits of bread into the cattle cars to be entertained by watching famished Jews fight over the food in an agonizing display of attempt at survival?

Here is Elie Wiesel's eyewitness account of just such an incident:

> In the wagon where the bread had fallen, a real battle had broken out. Men threw themselves on top of each other, stamping on each other, tearing at each other, biting each other. Wild beasts of prey, with animal hatred in their eyes; an extraordinary vitality had seized them, sharpening their teeth and nails.
>
> A crowd of workmen and curious spectators had collected along the train. They had probably never seen a train with such a cargo. Soon, nearly everywhere, pieces of bread were being dropped into the wagons. The

audience stared at these skeletons of men, fighting one another to the death for a mouthful.

A piece fell into our wagon. I decided that I would not move. Anyway, I knew that I would never have the strength to fight with a dozen savage men! Not far away I noticed an old man dragging himself along on all fours. He was trying to disengage himself from the struggle. He held one hand to his heart. I thought at first he had received a blow in the chest. Then I understood; he had a bit of bread under his shirt. With remarkable speed he drew it out and put it to his mouth. His eyes gleamed; a smile, like a grimace, lit up his dead face. And was immediately extinguished. A shadow had just loomed up near him. The shadow threw itself upon him. Felled to the ground, stunned with blows, the old man cried:

"Meir. Meir, my boy! Don't you recognize me? I'm your father . . . you're hurting me . . . you're killing your father! I've got some bread . . . for you too . . . for you too . . ."

He collapsed. His fist was still clenched around a small piece. He tried to carry it to his mouth. But the other one threw himself upon him and snatched it. The old man again whispered something, let out a rattle, and *died amid the general indifference. His son searched him, took the bread, and began to devour it.* He was not able to get very far. Two men had seen and hurled themselves upon him. Others joined in. When they withdrew, next to me were two corpses, side by side, the father and the son.

I was fifteen years old.

Night (New York, 1960), pp. 102-103.

So who were all of the people who cooperated with Hitler's master plan? They were in the thousands, perhaps in the millions. How many people does it take to exterminate 12,000,000 human beings, half of them Jews, half of them non-Jews? How many more does it take to close their eyes to what's happening—to be neutral, lukewarm who will be spewed forth on

Judgment Day according to their very own Christian tradition—in order to let the events continue?

One has only to think of the number of camps in order to begin to understand something of the magnitude of what went on. Here is as complete a listing as I can find—mostly taken from the *Encyclopedia Judaica* which has a seventy page entry on the Holocaust (the *Catholic Encyclopedia* has none). It is important to note that out of 146 camps listed, the number in Germany is but eighteen. We are not here concerned with something that Nazi Germany did alone, rather of that cosmic catastrophe performed in *Christian Europe*.

Austria	Ebensee, Gusen, Mauthausen
Belgium	Breendonck, Malines
Bulgaria	Somovit
Czechoslovakia	Novaky, Patronka, Petrzalka, Terezin, Zilina
Estonia	Aigali, Ereda, Goldfield, Kalevi, Klooga, Lagedi, Liiva, Vaivara
France	Agde, Argeles-sur-mer, Barcares, Beaune la Rodande, Camp du Richard, Compiegne, Drancy, Fort-Barraux, Gurs, Les Milles, Natzweiler-Struthof, Nexon, Pithiviers, Saint-Cyprien
Galicia	Borislav, Buchach, Lvov, Plaszow
Germany	Arbeitsdorf, Bergen-Belsen, Bochum, Brunswick, Buchenwald, Cottbus, Dachau, Dora, Esterwegen, Flossenburg, Grossrosen, Lichtenburg, Nevengamme, Niederhagen, Oranienburg, Ravensbruck, Sachsenhausen, Wells
Greece	Haidon
Hungary	Kistarcsa
Italy	Bolzano, Fossoli, Mantua, Raab

Latvia	Kaiserwald, Salaspils
Libya	Giado, Homs
Lichtenburg	Lichtenburg
Lithuania	Kaunas, Ponary
Netherlands	Amersfoort, Vught, Westerbork
Poland	Auschwitz, Belzec, Belzyce, Birkenau, Bogusze, Bronna Gora, Budzyn, Burggrabben, Chelmno, Chodosy, Chryzanow, Ciezanow, Elbing, Gerdaven, Heiligenbeil, Jaktorow, Jesau, Karczew, Kelbasin, Kielce, Kosaki, Lackie Wielkie, Majdanek, Miedzyrzec Podalski, Mielec, Mlyniewo, Nisko, Peikinia, Plew, Pomiechowek, Praust, Radomsko, Sasov, Schippenbeil, Seerapen, Skarzysko-Kamienna, Sobibor, Stolp, Stutthof, Thorn, Treblinka, Tyszowce, Zaglebia, Zaprudy, Zaslaw, Zawarnice, Zbaszyn
Rumania	Caracal, Markulesci
Russia	Akmechetka, Bogdanovka, Bratslav, Domanevka, Golta, Kamenka-Bugskaya, Koldychevo, Maly Trostinek, Odessa, Paczara, Sekiryani, Targu-Jiu, Tiraspol, Vapnyarka, Volkoysk, Yedintsy, Zborov
Yugoslavia	Ada, Djakovo, Jadovna, Jasenovac, Loborgrad, Saymishte

Nor were the camps enough to satisfy certain people. Here is an account of a survivor who returned home to Poland after having endured the brutalities of several different camps in which she was imprisoned. I had asked how she and her husband, who had also been incarcerated, but in another camp, had been reunited.

"After the war, in 1945, he was liberated in May. I was

liberated on the 25th of April, by the Elba. We didn't
know where to go. So we went home. Like everybody
thinks, well, we'll go home, back to Poland. And we
thought all of the people over there, the neighbors, will
greet us with open arms. You know *we survived!* I was
together with my sister and my mother, who had both
been in camp with me. When we were liberated, we saw
a long train going from Germany. We had nothing to
lose so we jumped on the train because we were harassed
from all sides—from the Russian soldiers, etc. So we
jumped on a freight train which was going toward
Poland. After a few days we arrived in our home town.
You know how we looked from the concentration camp.
But we had changed clothes. At the edge of town we
asked Polish people, 'Are there any Jews here?' They
said yes, there are a few back, but the minute they
recognized us as Jews, 'Why did you come back?' This is
the first thing they said to us as Jews. 'We thought that
you are dead. Why did you come back?' But they did tell
us where the few Jewish people were and we went there.
The city hall in our town gave the Jews a few
apartments in which to live—but concentrated in a few
places. Here were a couple of Jewish families in one
room. On another street there was a room with ten Jews.
They were afraid to go out. When we came we found
those families. One Jewish lady said to us, come and live
with me. I have two rooms and I'll give you one and I'll
have one. We were lucky to get that apartment. It was
like a garden apartment, three sides were apartments,
the fourth used by the Russian military as their
headquarters. This was in front of our apartment. We
were lucky to be living behind them.

"My husband, who thought as I did, came to the same
place, and we were reunited. We lived there until
September. I had been a dressmaker. I had learned
something. It's not like here. Here you think about
college. Over there we could only think about trades, to
make a living. So when we came back a lot of Polish

people brought me work to do. One morning a lady runs into us: 'My God, my God, you are alive. I am so happy that you are alive.' I said, 'What's happened?' She was all shaken. She said to us, 'Go away from here because they killed ten people in the apartment next to us—ten survivors.' Ten survivors. They survived the concentration camps, killed by the Polish people. Ten people in one house. The attackers killed them with pistols and a machine gun. One of the murderers was from the militia, and he got a machine gun. We were lucky because the Russian militia was right in front of us, so we were not attacked. We didn't run away, we went to find out what happened. We made a funeral for them. We all went to the cemetery with the Russian militia protecting us. *This was after the war in my home town.* We were afraid to go alone to the cemetery. A few weeks later we left our home town, then left Poland altogether. They found out who were the killers. A woman and two or three men. The woman was executed and I don't know what they did with the men."

The speaker's husband added this. "We were afraid because the hatred against Jews remained from before the war. We knew it would go on and on, the same thing. It was no use to be over there." When I asked the woman, later in our conversation, if she would wish ever to return to Poland, her answer was instantaneous "Never." Then she added, "Poland to me is blood."

It is of the greatest import that we Christians know precisely how Jews react to us after persecutions, pogroms, Inquisition, ghettoization, Holocaust, tragic events which indicate major points of history in Jewish-Christian relations. Perhaps Eliezer Berkovits put it most succinctly when he insisted, as a Jew, that "all we want of Christians is that they keep their hands off us and our children!" That has to be an immensely painful statement for Christians to confront. Who, us? we will

9

want to say. We who witness to the charity of Jesus Christ, the Lord and Savior of the world? It is supremely difficult for most of us to comprehend that we are seen as the persecutors, the torturers, the killers. But historically, that is how many Jews have perceived us. Again, it will be enlightening to compare entries in the *Catholic Encyclopedia* and the *Encyclopedia Judaica*. The former has a relatively long entry on "Baptism." The latter's article has a title which is significantly modified. It is "Baptism, Forced." There is evidence that when Christianity came to be established as the dominant religion in the Roman Empire, many Jews were forcibly baptized, even though official church teaching was that baptism had to be accepted willingly. The practice was so common that in the fifteenth century Pope Martin V had to forbid categorically the baptism of Jewish children under twelve without their parents' permission. After this, certain Christians tried to circumvent the decree by going to supreme lengths to prove that what they did was the result of persuasion rather than force. In 1747, Pope Benedict XIV ruled that once baptized, even against the proscriptions of canon law, a child was to be considered Christian, regardless. This helped to swell the number of kidnappings of Jewish children by zealous Christians, which children, once baptized, were lost to their families.

That, then, gives a hint of how *we* are perceived by some others. One must say "we" because as Christians we are not just whatever our own chronological ages are, rather we are each 2,000 years old, each a member of a mystical body of faith which shares in certain glories and therefore shares in certain responsibilities as well. If it is *our* Christianity which gave the artistic and intellectual impetus to the period of history known as the Renaissance, then it is our Christianity which also sponsored the Inquisition. If it is *our* Christianity which saved learning through what some have labeled the Dark Ages, then it is *our* Christianity which also counseled expropriation of Jewish property in various countries in various centuries. Here, for example, is Martin Luther. And keep in mind as you read this that these are not the words of some Nazi officer, caught up in the spirit of trying to rid the world of Jews in this century.

First, their synagogue or school is to be set on fire and what won't burn is to be heaped over with dirt and dumped on, so that no one can see a stone or chunk of it forever . . . Second, their houses are to be torn down and destroyed in the same way . . . Third, they are to have all their prayerbooks and Talmudics taken from them . . . Fourth, their rabbis are to be forbidden henceforth to teach, on penalty of life and limb . . . On penalty of life and limb, they are to be forbidden publicly to praise God, to thank (God), to pray (to God), to teach (of God) among us and ours . . . And furthermore, they shall be forbidden to utter the name of God in our hearing; no value shall be accorded the Jewish mouth (Maul) by us Christians, so that he may utter the name of God in our hearing, but whoever hears it from a Jew shall report him to the authorities or throw pig droppings on him . . . Fifth, the Jews are to be deprived totally of walkway and streets . . . Sixth, they are to be forbidden lending for interest and all the cash and holding of silver and gold are to be taken from them and put to one side for safe keeping . . . Seventh, the young, strong Jews and Jewesses are to have flail, axe and spade put into their hands.

Quoted by Franklin Littell in *The Crucifixion of the Jews* (New York, 1975), p. 105.

Earlier, there were the words of a man whom the Catholic Church considers one of its great ones, a saint.

HARRY JAMES CARGAS

These are from the person who has become known to religious history as the golden mouthed orator, St. John Chrysostom. Father Edward Flannery, in his book *The Anguish of the Jews*, says that St. John Chrysostom, "even in an age in which rhetorical denunciation [of Jews] was often indulged with complete abandon" unhappily "dwarfed" everyone else's record. Here are some of the words of the fourth century orator as quoted by Father Flannery:

How can Christians dare "have the slightest converse" with Jews, "most miserable of all men" (Homily 4:1), men who are " ... lustful, rapacious, greedy, perfidious bandits." Are they not "inveterate murderers, destroyers, men possessed by the devil" whom "debauchery and drunkenness have given them the manners of the pig and the lusty goat. They know only one thing, to satisfy their gullets, get drunk, to kill and maim one another ..." (1:4). Indeed, "they have surpassed the ferocity of wild beasts, for they murder their offspring and immolate them to the devil" (1:6). "They are impure and impious..." (1:4).

The Synagogue? Not only is it a theater and a house of prostitution, but a cavern of brigands, a "repair of wild beasts" (6:5), a place of "shame and ridicule" (1:3), "the domicile of the devil (1:6), as is also the souls of the Jews" (1:4, 6). Indeed Jews worship the devil; their rites are "criminal and impure;" their religion is "A disease" (3:1). Their synagogue, again, is "an assembly of criminals ... den of thieves ... a cavern of devils, an abyss of perdition" (1:2, 6:6).

God hates the Jews and always hated the Jews (6:4, 1:7), and on Judgment Day He will say to Judaizers, "Depart from Me, for you have had intercourse with My murderers." It is the duty of Christians to hate the Jews: "He who can never love Christ enough will never have done fighting against those [Jews] who hate Him" (7:1).

12

Flee, then, their assemblies, flee their houses, and far
from venerating the synagogue because of the books it
contains hold it in hatred and aversion for the same
reason" (1:5). Chrysostom himself gives the example:
"...I hate the synagogue precisely because it has the law
and prophets..." (6:6). "... I hate the Jews also because
they outrage the law..."

(New York, 1965), p. 48.

These virulent assaults are part of a pattern of
Christian anti-Judaism begun centuries before Chrysostom lived and continuing up to this very minute. They
are a part of Christian history. If we believe in a sense of
the mystical body, of what Teilhard de Chardin has
named the noosphere (that membrane of consciousness
which covers the universe, and in which we all partake),
of the Collective Unconscious of Carl Gustav Jung
(which gives the lie to the notion that we are born with a
tabula rasa, a mind clean as a slate, ready to receive all
totally new impressions)—if we have some grasp of any
or all of these, then we must at least vaguely comprehend what company some see us in as historical crimes
against the Jews are considered.

Given this, all of the foregoing, how many sermons,
homilies, lectures can any of us remember having heard
in church, about the Holocaust? It is over thirty-five
years since World War II has ended, over forty years
since Hitler began his program against Jews, with the
cooperation of so many. If we take merely the lesser
figure and suggest that given thirty-five years times
fifty-two Sundays (omitting other church days for the
sake of simple arithmetic) there are over one thousand
eight hundred sermon/homily opportunities for each of
us to hear *something* about one of the most significant
events in all of human history. I, personally, have not
heard one. I have heard preachings on why it is a sin for

13

men to wear Bermuda shorts, for example, but nothing even remotely hinting at the Holocaust as a possible theme.

The subject of this essay is precisely that. It is the Holocaust, begun with a capital letter because it is of a specific event which we write, a unique, one time, never before (and never again?) event which is perhaps ignored by many of us because it was so terrible and because it is so painful for us to face up to.

The number of Christians who have looked perseveringly at the subject is frighteningly small. They are there, and not to be ignored. Some of them will be quoted in these pages. Nevertheless the awareness of the relationship between Christianity and the Holocaust must be spread so that all Christians will know what many Jews do about Christianity, and that is that unless Christianity is revitalized, and soon, it too may have been among the victims at Auschwitz. It is certainly necessary to remember, as that magnificent Methodist Franklin Littell has underlined in his remarkable book *The Crucifixion of the Jews*, that Jesus and Paul and Peter would have perished at Auschwitz, a fact that latter-day gentile Christians dare not forget.

One problem with this vast subject is where to begin; another related difficulty is how to proceed. Perhaps a chronological approach to this history of Christian anti-Judaism is the logical starting point. We can proceed from then to now and end with hopeful and necessary projections/suggestions for the future. It seems appropriate at this point to insert a very prophetic poem by Wildred Owen, the British author who was killed near the very end of the First World War. It is a work with a much more powerful message than the author could have intended because the Holocaust could not have been known to him. And yet, given some knowledge of

Jewish-Christian interaction through the centuries . . .

THE PARABLE OF THE OLD MAN
AND THE YOUNG

So Abram rose, and clave the wood, and went,
And took the fire with him, and a knife.
And as they sojourned both of them together,
Isaac the first-born spake and said, "My Father,
Behold the preparations, fire and iron,
But where the lamb for this burnt-offering?"
Then Abram bound the youth with belts and straps,
And builded parapets and trenches there,
And stretched forth the knife to slay his son.
When lo! an angel called him out of heaven,
Saying, "Lay not thy hand upon the lad,
Neither do anything to him. Behold,
A ram, caught in a thicket by its horns;
Offer the Ram of Pride instead of him."
But the old man would not so, but slew his son,
And half the seed of Europe, one by one.

But we need to begin with earliest times. There was,
indeed, an anti-Judaism in pre-Christian days. Some
have seen the Exodus from Egypt by Israel as the first
pogrom. That took place some twelve hundred years
before Jesus' birth. About three centuries later the
dispersion of Jews began and through both forced and
voluntary exile from Palestine, Jewish communities
could be found, before Christ, in Babylonia, Egypt,
Mediterranean countries, Armenia, Persia, Spain and
Great Britain, among many nations. Problems with
Greeks, Egyptians, Romans and others have been documented by historians. Some of the famous names of the
ancient past have berated Jews, men like Seneca,
Cicero, Democritus, Tiberius, Trajan, Caligula, Quin-
tilian, Juvenal, Tacitus—a list much too long.

However, it is Christian anti-Judaism which must be
elaborated here, a distinctly unique kind of attack on

15

Judaism because of what has come to be known as the supersessionist theory. Briefly, this ideology contains the proclamation that the writings found in Jewish scriptures have been fulfilled in Christianity. The people of the Book have been told that henceforth their Book is obsolete. How may Christians today consider the fact that many Jews find the term "Old Testament" insulting to those of Jewish faith?

Here is Father Flannery again:

The first Christian Church, full of zeal and fervor, was a Jewish church in leadership, membership, and worship; and it remained within the precincts of the Synagogue. But as the universalist implications of the Gospel message (not yet fully written) made themselves felt, a series of developments gradually brought this arrangement to an end. In the tones of a prophet, Stephen charged the people and their leaders with infidelity to Moses as well as to the Messiah (Acts 7:2-7:53). By private revelation, Peter was instructed to accept the demi-proselyte, Cornelius, into the Church without committing him to the Law (Acts 10). The council of the apostles at Jerusalem decreed that gentile converts were not to be held to the legal observances (Gal. 2; Acts 15:11). Paul preached the inefficacy of the Law for both Jew and gentiles (Rom. 1:16, 2:10-11). Finally, at Antioch, Paul confronted Peter, insisting that while Jewish Christians might practice the Law, faith in Jesus Christ was necessary and sufficient for salvation (Gal. 2:11-21). This was the final disposition of the matter. Judaeo-Christianity, thus rejected, was destined to become a snare to Christian and Jew alike and a source of conflict for both Church and Synagogue.

(P. 26).

St. Paul, it seems, did not have a predominantly divisive outlook. While he noted that the law of the prophets was by way of preparation, and it was ended in Christ, he did not feel that God had somehow rejected

Judaism. Rather, in Romans 11:28-29, Paul indicated that ". . . as the chosen people, [Jews] are still loved by God, loved for the sake of their ancestors. God never takes back his gifts or revokes his choice." However, in that same epistle, Paul said some harsh things about Jews, and it is this latter attitude which has prevailed.

Littell points out that theological anti-Judaism began with the gentile converts of many tribes, with their natural resentment of the priority of Israel, their resistance to the authority of events in Jewish history, their pride in their own ethnic values, languages, cultures. Soon Jews came to be regarded as hypocrites, professing a false religion. Other Christian scriptures have been cited to indicate anti-Jewish bias, particularly in John's gospel, but such interpretation appears to be clearly incorrect. Nevertheless, the influence of such misinterpretation seems to have been great. (It is, incidentally, in John 4:22 that we read these words of Jesus, not located in Matthew, Mark or Luke: ". . . salvation comes from the Jews.")

Christian-Jewish hostility grew, with some persecutions being conducted by Jews against members of the newer religion. However, these were comparatively insignificant, mainly reactionary.

Church teachers kept up the assault now begun. Ignatius of Antioch, who died at the beginning of the second century, required that no Christians could keep the Jewish Sabbath, but must, of course, observe the newly appointed Lord's Day of Christianity. Ignatius also condescended, in Jewish eyes, to brand the prophets of Israel as Christians before their time and not, truly of the Jewish religion. This "take over" is part of the supersessionist approach to the older scriptures.

Nils Dahl has written that "The simplistic doctrine that Israel was rejected and the church chosen to be a new people of God is not really found within the New Testament, although it is adumbrated in some of the late writings."[1] Rosemary Ruether disagrees. She insists, in *Faith and Fratricide*, that the church won historical existence for herself by negating and claiming to supersede the historical existence of Israel. Only a new Christology, Reuther believes, offers a way out of anti-Judaism for Christians.

The answer is not a clear one, indeed the question may not be. Nevertheless, what has proven to be historically evident is exemplified by the title of Jules Isaac's very important volume, published in 1964, *The Teaching of Contempt: The Christian Roots of Anti-Semitism.* Isaac was a French Jew, a historian, who lost his wife, daughter and other family members in the Holocaust. He spent the final twenty-three years of his life studying the answer to the question of specifically Christian guilt in the massacre of the six million Jewish victims of the Holocaust. He concluded that a true Christian cannot be at once precisely that and anti-Jewish. However, he also concluded that anti-Judaism is profoundly rooted in Christianity. Isaac wrote that from the time of early conflict with Judaism, the Christian church propagated three treacherous lies, what he calls the "three main themes of the teaching of contempt." They are 1) in the year 70 A.D. the dispersion of the Jews took place as a punishment by God for their infidelity; 2) at the time of Christ, Judaism was in an unhealthy, degenerate state; 3) the Jewish people are guilty of having killed God. To see how this has persisted we need only to read Michael Dov Weissmandl's account of a conversation with a Papal Nuncio in 1944, at the height of the Holocaust persecutions, wherein the church official is reported to have said this: "There is no innocent blood of Jewish children in the world. All Jewish blood is guilty. You have to die. This is the punishment that has been awaiting you because of that sin [deicide]."[2] (This, of course, makes Hitler a wonderful instrument of God's justice, does it not?)

St. Justin was probably the first to proclaim that because Jews killed Christ, they had been made to suffer. He said to a rabbi that the "tribulations were justly imposed upon you, for you have murdered the Just One." This bad theology and bad history have been promulgated ever since by people calling themselves Christians.

In the third century St. Cyprian proved equally as anti-Judaic. First he says that Jesus was put to death by the Jews and then insists that "Now the peoplehood of the Jews has been cancelled," a statement which could be used to justify the intimidation and even slaughter of Jews for seventeen more centuries. Another third century figure, also sainted, Hippolytus, said that all that the Jews had done had been pardonable but now they would be left in despair "because they killed the Son of their Benefactor."

Now we approach the fourth century and the first of three Western anti-Jewish policies as defined by Raul Hilberg in his monumental volume, *The Destruction of the European Jews.* (He notes, by the way, that while pre-Christian Rome crushed the independent Jewish state of Judea, Rome had no anti-Jewish policy and in fact Jews who lived in Rome itself enjoyed equality under the law.) Hilberg says that at this point, wherein the state carried out the policies of the church, twelve centuries of proscribed measures for Jews, by the Catholic church, the Jews were indeed subject to such policies in Christendom. (The other two policies of the West applied against Jewry in its disposal include expulsion—which began as an alternative but developed into a goal of anti-Judaic activity—and the final policy as starkly put: to kill the Jews.) In Hilberg's words: "To summarize: Since the fourth century after Christ, there have been three anti-Jewish policies: conversion, expulsion, annihilation. The second appeared as an alternative to the first, and the third emerged as an alternative to the second." (New York, 1973), p. 3.

This fourth century, which Father Flannery calls "critical" in Jewish-Christian history, is filled with abusive attacks by churchmen. This was the time when Christianity became the state religion and came to have heavy clout, politically. How church members regarded their apparent adversaries, their rivals, the Jews, can be seen from the following.

Eusebius of Caesarea distinguished between Hebrews (seen as primitive Christians) and Jews (less enlightened). The patriarchs were considered to be in the former group in this displacement or supersessionist view. Hilary of Poitiers saw Jewish history as proving that the Jews are perpetually perverse. St. Ephraim called the Synagogue a "harlot" while Cyril of Jerusalem and Epiphanius, each with the honored title of saint, also wrote pejoratively about Jews. Another saint, Gregory of Nyssa, called Jews "slayers of the Lord, murderers of the prophets, enemies of God, haters of God, adversaries of grace, enemies of their fathers' faith, advocates of the devil, brood of vipers, slanderers, scoffers, men of darkened minds, leaven of the Pharisees, congregation of demons, sinners, wicked men, stoners, and haters of goodness" (Flannery, p. 47). St. Jerome continues the attack, seeing Jews as "serpents," saying that their image is found in Judas and contending that their psalms and prayers are "the braying of donkeys."

In this atmosphere of hatred lived and preached John

Chrysostom, characterized by Flannery as a man "who, up to his time, stands without peer or parallel in the entire literature *Adversus Judaeos*." As Flannery concludes, "Christians as well as Jews can only deplore these sermons" (p. 49). St. Augustine saw the Jews as existing to serve Christians.

Much else occurred during this century including church councils which prohibited Christians from marrying Jews and barred Christians from celebrating the Passover with Jews. There were some measures promulgated to assist Jews to preserve certain rights but these were restrained, to say the minimal, in comparison with what was preached and practiced against Jews. In effect many were forced out of agriculture and industry and into small trades. None could participate in public functions, the military, or administrative positions. At this time, too, physical attacks against Jews increased, involving the citizenry on "their" level comparable to what the church Fathers taught on "theirs."

As the centuries passed, there was more of the same. With them came forced baptisms of Jews, (though opposed by Pope St. Gregory and official church policy) and Judaism was increasingly seen by many as a corrupt religion. In seventh century Spain children of Jews were baptized and taken from their parents for a Christian education. Expulsion of Jews became more common, and we are reminded of Hilberg's second policy of anti-Judaism effected by Western civilization. Forced conversions, particularly in nations like France, became the rule. In the eighth and ninth centuries, under Pepin and Charlemagne, conditions improved for Jews and were particularly advanced under Charlemagne's son Louis the Pious.

However this did not last. The archbishop of Lyons,

21

St. Abrogard, wrote a pair of treatises, the titles of which only partially indicate their virulence: *On the Insolence of Jews* and *On Jewish Superstitions*. By the tenth century, Jewish property began to be expropriated. Furthermore, a custom grew up where on Good Fridays, in retribution for the crucifixion, a local Jew received a symbolic blow on his face from a Church official. Thus continued and passed on was the convenience of blaming others for the death of Jesus who, according to church teachings, died because all, *including Christians*, were sinners and thus all had responsibility in Jesus' death.

The end of the eleventh century, 1096 precisely, is a major catastrophic time in Jewish history. This was the year of the infamous First Crusade. Let us look at the Crusade from a Jewish point of view:

The Crusades and their attendant degradation were firmly imprinted on the historic consciousness of the Jews. This period became singled out in the popular mind as the start of and explanation for the misfortunes of the Jews, although in fact the excesses were only symptomatic of a process which had already been set in motion earlier. The Crusades marked in various ways a turning point in the history of the Western world, and this was reflected also in Jewish history. Indeed, it is from this point only that the history of the Jews in the Rhineland and Central Europe may be said to acquire continuity; whereas before the general picture has had to be constructed from scattered fragments and documents, henceforth the record is more or less sustained and complete. As in the case to some extent with general historiography, it is only at this period, with the remarkably graphic and moving records of the Rhineland massacres in 1096, that consistent Jewish historiography, or at least chronography, begins to be preserved, even though there are fragmentary records written earlier. The history that now unfolded was

predominantly a tragic one. Whereas in European
Jewish history before this date episodes of violence and
persecution are occasionally known, there now began a
period of intermittently recurring massacre and persecution which colored European Jewish experience for
centuries to come. The heightened religiosity of the age
resulted in the sharpening of the system of anti-Jewish
discrimination and of Jewish humiliation, culminating
in the legislation of the Fourth Lateran Council of 1215.
The chronicles of Solomon b. Samson, Eliezer b. Nathan
of Mainz, Ephraim b. Jacob of Bonn, Eleazar b. Judah of
Worms, and many others whose names are not known,
described the events of the Crusades, the scenes of the
massacres, and the martyrs. They are also to be
regarded as basic sources from which statistical
accounts of the Crusades must start. Through capturing
these events they magnified their significance, but
thereby furnished an ideal of conduct which was
constantly recalled to mind whenever severe persecutions befell the Jews.

(*Encyclopedia Judaica*)

Note the clearly different emphasis of the article on
the Crusades in the *Catholic Encyclopedia* from this, its
concluding paragraph:

The Crusades represented an effort of the greatest
magnitude. Christians in the Middle Ages consented to
enormous sacrifices for what they regarded as a sacred
obligation: the defense of their brethren in danger and
the liberation of the Holy Land hallowed by the footsteps
of Christ. The Crusades were not an act of intolerance:
they aimed neither at the forced conversion of non-
Christian nor at the massacre of "infidels." These
expeditions had, indeed, military, financial, and economical aspects, but above all else they can be characterized as a penitential act and voluntary effort in the
service of God. The notion of bearing arms in God's
service, though it may seem paradoxical, was perfectly

attuned to the mentality of the Middle Ages and, in the last analysis, assured the success of the Crusades. The concept of devoting cosiderable effort to a task in the service of God guarantees lasting favor to the Crusade idea as applied in our day to the works of peace.

The thirteenth century Doctor of the Church, St. Thomas Aquinas, wrote this: "It would be licit, according to custom, to hold Jews, because of their crime, in perpetual servitude, and therefore the princes may regard the possession of Jews as belonging to their state; however they may use them with moderation and not deprive Jews of things necessary to life" (in Flannery, p. 95). Later, this became law. As one jurist wrote, "The Jew cannot have anything of his own. Whatever he acquires he acquires not for himself but for the king" (in Flannery, p. 95). By the end of the thirteenth century Jews were forced out of France, England, and most of Germany.

The next dismal chapter is one of the most incredible of all. It is the period which brought on the accusation of what is called Ritual Murder. The charge seems to have been first seriously aimed at Jews in the twelfth century. Ritual murder, initially, was said to be the sacrifice by Jews of a Christian victim, most usually a child, during the Christian Holy Week, for religious purposes. But this was too restrictive. Soon, any murder of a Christian which was determined to be for some supernatural end was considered in this category. The first charge occurred in England but it spread to many European nations. Many Jews were massacred in retaliation. Some of the Christian "victims" became, without foundation, popularly venerated by other Christians. The finding of a dead Christian child, regardless of circumstances, might be enough to raise the collective Christian voice of a community against Jews. Actually, such accusations against Jews were absurd, given Jewish doctrine and practice which included an abomination of bloodletting, and at least four popes insisted on the innocence of Jews of these practices. But the denunciations, incredible as they were, continued. Who could believe it? A Catholic priest and historian, Father Vacandard, has established that not a single case of ritual murder has ever been historically proven. Pope Innocent III's Fourth Lateran Council decreed that Jews (and Saracens) had to wear distinctive clothing, a full seven and a half centuries before the Nazis required the yellow star as Jewish garb. The burning of the Talmud by Christians was done, people were threatened with excommunication for consulting Jewish physicians and perhaps 100,000 Jews were killed in Germany and Austria in 1298 because of the unfounded charge that a Jew had desecrated a communion host. Tales of smaller scale massacres abound and many Jews, faced with forced baptism, chose suicide rather than betray their faith. In the fifteenth century, another saint, the Franciscan John Capistrano, earned his title "scourge of the Jews" and he became one of the Inquisitors of the Jews. The Inquisition, of course, has been seen, finally, as one of the most tragic periods in Christianity's history.

In about the middle of the twelfth century, Christians came to believe increasingly in the efficacy of force to gain ecclesiastical unity. It reached such a point that in several regions, the death penalty was decreed for heresy. Because he feared the charge of heresy would be abused for political motives, Pope Gregory IX, in 1231, required that only the church could try heretics and he then instituted the papal Inquisition. The Inquisitors had great power, not the least incidental of which was the naming of deputies who shared in that power. Since political rulers could themselves be denounced, the Inquisition was widely supported by the civil authorities. Death penalties, sometimes preceded by extreme tortures, were adminstered against victims. Jews who had been forced to be baptized but remained loyal to Judaism were persecuted, particularly in Spain, through the Inquisition. In Spain the oppression was especially widespread and caused much anguish even to Jews who had not converted and were technically outside of the Inquisition's domain.

The Reformation period followed—with little improvement, at least in attitude by Christians toward the Jews. Luther was quoted earlier. Here is more from him:

> Herewith you can readily see how they understand and obey the fifth commandment of God, namely, that they are thirsty bloodhounds and murderers of all Christendom, with full intent, now for more than fourteen hundred years, and indeed they were often burned to death upon the accusation that they had poisoned water and wells, stolen children, and torn and hacked them apart, in order to cool their temper secretly with Christian blood.

In the sixteenth century, Pope Paul IV acted in such a way that Flannery has judged that "There are few popes who compare with him for severity toward Jews" (p. 154). In 1700 Johann Eisenmenger published *Entdectes Judentum* (Judaism Unmasked) which has been an inspired encyclopedia of anti-Judaism until now.

For various reasons Jews moved into ghettos and were separated from the rest of the citizens. In some areas this actually led to their protection and helped their survival, although this was not the intent of those who decreed and enforced the ghettoizations. But as time passed, many ghettos began to pass also, and as the nineteenth century opened, emancipation of Jews became a gradual reality. The reasons are complex and

irrelevant for our purposes here. Some were of an
internal, Jewish nature, while others had a broader
basis. The French and American revolutions are
important here. But anti-Judaism was not absent.
German thinkers like Friedrich Schleiermacher,
Johann Fichte and Johann Wolfgang von Goethe were
vocal about their negative attitudes toward Jews and
the influential Karl Marx, himself born a Jew but
baptized as a child, wrote this, among other passages:

> What is the object of the Jew's worship in this world?
> Usury. What is his worldly God? Money. Very well then;
> emancipation from usury and money, that is, from
> practical, real Judaism, would constitute the emancipa-
> tion of our time . . . The emancipation of society from
> Jewry.
>
> (Flannery, p. 67.)

Nevertheless the cause of political emancipation of
Jews was advanced in the world. But, as Flannery
indicates, while this was an important improvement in
the situation of Jews, the blessing was not unaccom-
panied by certain reversals. "Instead of disappearing,
anti-Semitism merely changed its guise. An old form
was on the wane, another in the making. The theological
bias was fainter but the national, economic, and ethnic
resentments were stronger. Less noted as a 'deicide
people,' Jews became abhorred as supposedly unassimi-
lable economic parasites. Clearly, their emancipation
had a proviso attached: that they dissolve in the gentile
melting pot" (Flannery, p. 173).

Of course the chronology suggested here is too neat to
be entirely accurate. Non-theological anti-Judaism may
be said to have begun as early as two centuries
previously, in the seventeenth. Names like Baruch
Spinoza, himself a Jew, Voltaire, Diderot, Hegel,
Proudhon, and many others are powerful here. They led

up to one of the most infamous of all, Arthur de Gobineau who, in his *Essay on the Inequality of Human Races,* advocated Aryan supremacy and Semitic inferiority. Jews, in de Gobineau's view, were especially inferior to German Aryans. It was published in 1884. In just half a century, Hitler would try to purge the world of these inferior beings and de Gobineau's "scientific" findings were among the foundation points of the Fuehrer's policy. Nor was de Gobineau alone in his teachings; nor was Germany alone infected by such thought. In France the infamous Dreyfus affair, in which a Jewish officer was framed as a German spy, brought anti-Judaism into the open again. Although the perpetrators of the crime were exposed (one who forged documents implicating Dreyfus committed suicide), and although Dreyfus was ultimately and absolutely cleared (not without incredible difficulties), latent anti-Judaism became openly that. Catholics in France, as symbolized by the Catholic press of that nation, disgraced themselves in their show of feelings towards Jews catalyzed by the Dreyfus case. All over Europe, anti-Judaic attitudes were being expressed.

The time was opportune then, for the publication in 1905, of a book called *The Protocols of the Learned Elders of Zion.* This volume is purported to be a series of two dozen lectures by influential Jews on how to subjugate the world to Jewish control—the international Jewish conspiracy hoax, if you will. *The Protocols* was proven to be a forgery, but became very influential, was promulgated as true by Henry Ford and has even been cited recently by certain Arab diplomats in the United Nations as evidence of a Jewish plot to take over the world. The exposure of the fraud came in 1921, but to this hour *The Protocols* remains fodder for anti-Judaists who refuse to recognize the truth on this matter.

World War I proved tragic for Jews. While they fought in the armies of their respective nations, they were not trusted and predictably, when the war ended, they were branded as unwilling participants, particularly (and unjustly) in Germany. Polish armies probably murdered some thirty thousand Jews (President Woodrow Wilson interceded to help stop the slaughter), 200,000 Rumanian Jews lost their citizenship and in Hungary, and in Austria, and in Turkey . . . Jews everywhere were separated from other citizens. How were they to react, then, when Hitler's onslaught began? To whom could they turn for assistance, for compassion? They were left almost entirely isolated and helpless. As Raul Hilberg has shrewdly indicated about this period, Hitler did not have to originate any propaganda or invent any laws. He did not have to create a machine. All he had to do was rise to personal power. The stage was, indeed, set for him. All it needed was a star performer. Here are words from a German Cardinal, Michael von Faulhaber, spoken in a 1933 sermon, which gave inaccurate theological support to so much of the prejudice against Jews:

> After the death of Christ Israel was dismissed from the service of Revelation. She did not know the time of her visitation. She had repudiated and rejected the Lord's Anointed, had driven him to the Cross. . . . The Daughters of Zion received the bill of divorce and from that time forth Assuerus wanders, forever restless, over the face of the earth.[3]

Actually, however, it appears that Christian anti-Judaism was less destructive than racial anti-Judaism as we approach the period of the Holocaust. This is in no way meant to mitigate the blame against any form of such hatred, but it is interesting to note the major line of discussion in a book by the distinguished Jewish scholar Uriel Tal, *Christians and Jews in Germany: Religion, Politics and Ideology in the Second Reich, 1870-1914.* Here, basically, although caricatured, are Professor Tal's conclusions: Tension arose from the unwillingness of Germans to allow Jews to be integrated into the state while Jews attempted, at the same time, to retain a certain separateness. From a theological viewpoint, Judaism was seen as an anachronism, replaced by the New Dispensation. Liberal Jews felt that Liberal Protestants really accepted Judaism's basic opposition to Christianity and reduced religion to ethics, reduced theological mysteries to anthropology, therefore denying the dogma of the church. As Tal wrote, it is clear that it was the non-Christian and anti-Christian character of racial-political anti-Judaism that proved to be the greatest obstacle to its development. However, after World War I the non-Christian anti-Christian character of anti-Judaism grew stronger and this removed a main obstacle to the spread of *racial* anti-Judaism. Tal continues by saying that Christian anti-Judaism was not as virulent as its racial counterpart. It permitted Jews to exist (though not flourish) as the living witness to the truth of Christianity. The Jew has to remain in order to act out the role of villain in the drama of salvation, and the Jew could, after all, be converted, baptized. But according to racial anti-Judaism, nothing could penetrate the tainted Jewish seed. The Jew must be destroyed. Racial anti-Judaism put its faith in the efficacy of blood. It is important to Tal's thesis to note that, while racial anti-Judaism was a worse brand, the history of Christianity provided the rationale for violence against Jews. We are ready, now, for the third of the Western policies against the Jews, according to Hilberg. Kill them.

Jews have asked, and continue to ask: Where was God at Auschwitz? Why aren't more Christians asking that question, too? Jewish survivor Elie Wiesel told me in a television interview that he believes that "the sincere Christian knows that what died in Auschwitz was not the Jewish people but Christianity." Wiesel went on to say that Pope John XXIII, whom Wiesel knew, saw this and therefore called the Second Vatican Council into existence—perhaps Wiesel would say in an attempt at a resurrection.

However that may be, we must insist with Arthur Hertzberg who, in viewing what theologian Robert E. Willis has called "the indisputable success of the Nazi program" has asked, ". . . is it conceivable that the enormous power of this hatred was bred in a few short decades?"[4] The answer is obvious. We as inheritors of the traditions of the members of the Mystical Body, as participants in the noosphere, as constituents of the collective unconscious, need to recognize this.

Perhaps, for a period at least, we need to modify a traditional question as we try to gain perspective on history, on events. Many of us have been taught to judge relevance by asking: What is this in the light of eternity? For a time, let us put it this way: What is this in the light of the flames of Auschwitz, the period in history when humanity ratified Hell?

31

II
THE NAZI ATROCITIES

Jewish theologian Irving Greenberg regards the Holocaust as an unprecedented challenge to both Judaism and Christianity. It radically contradicts, he believes, the central affirmation of both faiths. In the light of the great cruelties of World War II, and particularly of the attempted annihilation of a people, how can we say that we are made in God's image? How can we believe that human life is infinitely precious? "Both religions have always sought to isolate their central events—Exodus and Easter—from further revelations or from the challenge of the demonic counter-experience of evil in history. By and large, both religions have continued since 1945 as if nothing had happened to change their central understanding. It is increasingly obvious that this is impossible, that the Holocaust cannot be ignored."[1]

We are after all, if nothing else, reflecting on the murder of 1,000,000 Jewish children. We have mentioned how the Nazi attitude was a kind of giant step of logical progression based on a long and sorrowful history of political, religious and racial anti-Judaism. Even some of the Nazi tactics were not very original. Nazis demanded the protection of Aryan blood from defilement by Jewish blood. But the Synod of Elvira, in the year 306, prohibited intermarriage and sexual intercourse between Christians and Jews. In 535 the Synod of Clermont decreed that Jews could not hold public office. In 538 Jews were forbidden to show themselves in the streets during Passion Week. The list is long, the list is embarrassing: Jews not permitted to take Christians to court or be witnesses against Christians in a trial (1179); Jewish clothes had to be marked with a badge (1215); compulsory ghettoization of Jews (1267); Christians could not engage in real estate transactions with Jews (1279); Jews not allowed to earn academic degrees (1434). This is only a partial roster of events which have their parallels in Nazi practices. All of this and so pitifully much more provides a background for the attempted annihilat:on of world Jewry—in which so many Christians were active, and during which so many Christians were passive.

There were, as we know, theoretical bases used to rationalize what was to be done. There was *Rassenkunde*, racial science, based primarily on the work of Arthur de Gobineau (d. 1882) who insisted that the racial question overshadows all other problems of history, that it holds the key to them all, and that the inequality of the races from whose fusion a people is formed is enough to explain the whole course of its destiny. There are the writings of Johann Fichte (d. 1814) who has been called the father of both German nationalism and modern German anti-Judaism. There are the ideas of German composer Richard Wagner (d. 1883) whose racist concepts were influenced by de Gobineau (who was French) and Houston Stewart Chamberlain (who was English). Wagner was pleased to learn from the former that the Germans were probably the best of all the Aryans, from the latter that Jewish influence could best be combated through Teutonic cultural development. Chamberlain also argued that the Germans had inalienable right to be masters of the world. Wagner was a strong, unrelenting Jew hater best characterized, perhaps, by this statement: "The Jew is the plastic demon of the decline of mankind." There is also the influence of social Darwinism on Nazi theory, of Goethe's Faust, with his overreaching will, as Nora Levin has indicated, and she has also noted that "Wotan willing his own destruction and Tristan and Isolde, dying in an ecstasy of love, are significantly German."

The Holocaust (New York, 1973), pp. 7-8.

Germany was saturated in a certain atmosphere. In 1925-27, when the German Republic was more stable than it ever was to have been, rioting against Jews grew, as did the desecration of Jewish cemeteries. Legislation against Jews was constantly introduced in the national and local legislatures. During this period over 700 racist, anti-Jewish newspapers were published throughout the country. Even in children's books passages like this could be read: "Without solution of the Jewish question / No salvation of mankind."

The portrait of the Jew which emerged from all of this was clearly a contradictory one. On one side the Jew was presented as subhuman, as contemptible, as a mere pestilence to be eradicated. However, the second view, of the Jew as "the mythic omnipotent superadversary" was also promulgated. It seemed to be an either/or situation but in the German mind, if we can allude to such a concept, it was not. In either instance, facing the Jew as disease or the Jew as super enemy, something needed to be done. Someone was needed who would lead the fight against the Jew. Onto the scene came a redeemer. After a humiliating loss in the First World War (blamed on Jews by some) and an even more humiliating peace treaty, the person who could convince a significant number of Germans that he would unite Germany, return to it a rightful prestige and at the same time rid it of the cause of its troubles—the Jew— would be regarded as a savior. Onto the scene came Adolf Hitler. Here was the magnetic personality who could convince people that "by defending myself against the Jew, I am fighting for the work of the Lord." Here is a man of whom a German Christian, a Dr. Engelke, had said, "God has manifested himself not in Jesus Christ but in Adolf Hitler." Hanns Kerrl, Minister for Church Affairs, had these words in 1937: "A new authority has

risen as to what Christ and Christianity really are—
Adolf Hitler." Kerrl even went beyond this. "As Christ
in his twelve disciples raised a stock fortified unto
martyrdom, so in Germany today we are witnessing the
same thing . . . Adolf Hitler is the true Holy Ghost!"[2]
Hitler was born in 1889 in Austria. He proved a poor
student and his academic failures irritated him for
many succeeding years. He enjoyed reading the Nordic
tales of gods and heroes and particularly was addicted
to the writings of Karl May, an ex-convict author who
had never been to the Wild West but who wrote action
tales set in that region. These works featured a hero
called Old Shatterhand, an American who thrived on
killing Indians who, he considered, were members of an
inferior race. Hitler was to model himself after Old
Shatterhand. It is known that Hitler continued to read
May's literature (which was aimed at a juvenile
audience) while conducting the war against Russia and
he sometimes referred to the Soviets as "Redskins." The
future Fuehrer fought in World War I, was seriously
wounded and received several decorations. In 1919,
when the German Worker's Party was founded, he
became its fifty-fifth member. Before long he was
appointed its head of propaganda and publicity. And he
showed himself to be an especially effective speaker.
Early in 1921 the first great Nazi mass meeting was
held in Munich and Hitler was made first chairman of
the National Socialist German Workers' Party
(NSDAP). Some three months later, on November 4,
1921, a private army, the SA (storm troopers) was
instituted. Descriptively identified as the Brownshirts,
these guards at Nazi meetings were later used to battle
Communists and others in the streets. By 1932 there
were 400,000 men in the SA.

In late 1923 Hitler made a move to seize power in

Bavaria with the so-called Beer Hall *Putsch* in Munich. This attempted coup failed and Hitler was arrested, put on trial and convicted. During the trial, the defendant made a deep impression on certain Germans before he was sentenced to five years in prison (of which he served eight and a half months). It was while imprisoned that he began dictating his book, *Mein Kampf* (My Fight), to friends. Millions of copies were sold throughout the world and Hitler became rich on the royalties. Here, for our purposes, are some quotations from *Mein Kampf* (New York, 1971): The Jews' "whole existence is an embodied protest against the aesthetics of the Lord's image" (p. 178). "Was there any form of filth or profligacy, particularly in cultural life, without at least one Jew involved in it?" (p. 57). "The foremost connoisseurs of this truth regarding the possibilities in the use of falsehood and slander have always been the Jews; for after all, their whole existence is based on one single great lie, to wit, that they are a religious community while actually they are a race—and what a race!" (p. 232). "Existence impels the Jew to lie, and to lie perpetually, just as it compels the inhabitants of the northern countries to wear warm clothing" (p. 305). "The Jew has always been a people with definite racial characteristics and never a religion; only in order to get ahead he early sought for a means which could distract unpleasant attention from his person" (p. 306). Hitler cites the fraudulent *Protocols of the Learned Elders of Zion* to support his case, he rants against pacifism as "Jewish nonsense," he insists that no Jew could be a German, Jews are inferior beings and much, much more. His attack became so broad that Hitler confidently wrote this: "And so the Jew today is the great agitator for the complete destruction of Germany. Wherever in the world we read of attacks against

Germany, Jews are their fabricators, just as in peace-
time and during War the press of the Jewish stock
exchange and Marxists systematically stirred up hatred
against Germany until state after state abandoned
neutrality and, renouncing the true interests of the
peoples, entered the service of the World War coalition"
against Germany (p. 623).

Hitler left prison in December, 1924. Less than three
months later, a reconstituted NSDAP gained fewer
than a quarter of a million votes out of twenty seven
million cast. A month later Field Marshall Paul von
Hindenburg became the second President of the
Weimar Republic. The next year, a Party day was held
in Nuremberg at which 30,000 Brownshirts marched.
In 1928, in Reichstag elections, Nazis gained only 2.5%
of the vote. In early 1929, Heinrich Himmler became
head of Hitler's blackshirted personal guard, the SS or
elite guard. In August of the same year, Party day
attracted 150,000 participants. The next year, in
Reichstag elections, the Nazi share of votes rose to 18%;
SS and SA activities grew more bold. In presidential
elections in 1932, Hitler received 13.7 million votes.
Hindenburg was reelected President of the Republic
and on January 30th of the next year Hitler was
appointed Chancellor of the Republic. Soon he gained
emergency powers by presidential decree and in new
elections, Nazis gained 288 seats out of 647 deputies.
Himmler and Joseph Goebbels grew in power as did
Rudolf Hess. On April 26 (1933) the Gestapo force was
formed. In November of that year the Nazi party
received 93% of the vote cast in the Reichstag election.

In August of 1934, President von Hindenburg died.
Hitler declared himself the Fuehrer of Germany, a
move ratified by a vote of approval of nearly 90% of
those casting ballots less than three weeks afterwards.

A year later, official steps were taken to disenfranchise Jews in what have become known to history as the Nuremberg Laws on Citizenship and Race. Here is a paragraph by Louis L. Snyder describing these laws:

The Nuremberg Laws were designed by Hitler to define the status of Jews in Germany and to restrict them in political and social life. In his drive for political power Hitler promoted a bitter anti-Semitic campaign and stirred up extreme hatred against the Jews. After becoming Chancellor, he encouraged his followers to assault and beat Jews, to humiliate them by forcing them to clean the streets, to picket or close Jewish businesses, and to denounce Jews in the professions as rogues, profiteers, and traitors. When accounts of Nazi atrocities were published abroad, a boycott of German goods was urged in retaliation. The result was disastrous for German Jews. Jewish businesses were boycotted, Jewish physicians excluded from hospitals, Jewish judges dismissed, and Jewish students thrown out of the universities. Jews were increasingly barred from all German life. "The Jew can speak only Jewish. When he writes in German, he lies." From September to November 1935 Hitler took steps to define the legal status of Jews in Germany. The Nuremberg Laws withdrew German citizenship from persons of "non-German blood."[3]

German audacity continued to increase. So did Italian, and during 1936 the two nations grew together on an official level. In 1937 Pope Pius XI was concerned enough to issue an encyclical letter "With Deep Anxiety," which protested against German violations of natural law and justice. This letter was not a strong statement on behalf of Jews, and historians have lamented this. However what is little known is the fact that another statement had been planned, *and in fact was written* for Pius XI, which could possibly have changed a significant part of the history of World War

41

II. It is best to tell the story of this tragedy as I first did in another book.

As I prepare this manuscript for publication the *National Catholic Reporter*, a totally lay-edited newspaper, breaks a tragic story about an unpublished papal encyclical letter on anti-Semitism, a letter which, had it been circulated, might have had an immense effect on the prosecution and persecutions of World War II. Pope Pius XI commissioned a U.S. Jesuit priest, John LaFarge, to write an encyclical for the Pope, attacking racism and anti-Semitism. The request was made in June, 1938, a full fifteen months before the outbreak of the Second World War. Through a series of apparently Machiavellian machinations, the message never got into print. After examining the evidence, an editorial writer for the *National Catholic Reporter* indicated that, "Considering all this, we must conclude that the publication of the encyclical draft at the time it was written may have saved hundreds of thousands, perhaps millions, of lives."

I wish I could say the story is incredible. But I have read Church history and it is all *too* believable. Father LaFarge wrote *Humani Generis Unitas (The Unity of the Human Race)* as requested but apparently his Jesuit Superior General, a Polish count, Father Wlodimir Ledochowski, withheld the completed manuscript from the Pope for what NCR concluded were "political reasons." Pius XI's death the following February doomed the anti-Semitic declaration to limbo. (Cardinal Jean Tisserant, a close associate of the Pope, claimed that Pius XI was poisoned by a physician, Dr. Francesco Petacci, whose daughter Clara was Mussolini's mistress. The Pope died on the eve of a scheduled speech to Italian bishops which was to have been an attack on Fascism.) When the successor Pope, Pius XII, published his first encyclical—using the title of LaFarge's work—the sections on racism and anti-Semitism were not included. Here is Jim Castelli's account as it appears in the NCR:

The anti-Semitism section entitled, "The Jews and
Anti-Semitism (Religious Separation)" directly fol-
lows the racism section. It begins by saying, "It
becomes clear that the struggle for racial purity
ends by being uniquely the struggle against Jews."
The encyclical draft said contemporary anti-Semitism
has historical roots:

"Save for the systematic cruelty, this struggle, in
true motives and methods, is no different from
persecutions everywhere carried out against the
Jews from antiquity. These persecutions have been
censured by the Holy See on more than one
occasion, but especially when they have worn the
mantle of Christianity."

The following paragraphs described the "actual persecution of the Jews":

"As a result of such a persecution, millions of
persons are deprived of the most elementary rights
and privileges of citizens in the very land of their
birth. Denied legal protection against violence and
robbery, exposed to every form of insult and public
degradation, innocent people are treated as criminals though they have circumspectly obeyed the
law of their native land.

"Even those who in time of war fought bravely
for their country are treated as traitors, and the
children of those who laid down their lives in their
country's behalf are branded as outlaws by the very
fact of their parentage. The values of patriotism, so
loudly invoked for the benefit of one class of
citizens, are ridiculed when invoked for others who
come under the racial ban.

"In the case of the Jews, this flagrant denial of
human rights sends many thousands of helpless
persons out over the face of the earth without any
resources. . . ."

There's more, but it is difficult to continue. Another
Catholic lay publication, the magazine *Commonweal*,

editorialized about the scandal: ". . . there is no evading
the past; it is true that many Christians were all-too-
ready to co-operate in the persecution of the Jews, and it
is this fact, even more than the silence of Pius XII, that
stains the collective conscience of Christians. History is
dealing harshly with Pius XII on this issue and rightly
so, but on this side of the Atlantic as well as the other he
was not alone in keeping silence."[4]

This last is a great point. Too many people remained
silent, perhaps did not want to get involved. The charge
weighs heavily against first German and later many
other intellectuals. Nora Levin has written of "the
general world indifference that prevailed through the
agony of Europe's Jews" (p. 143). We know that there
was no significant protest; a German battlecry became
famous: "Hep! Hep! Hep! Death and Destruction to all
the Jews." Few reacted negatively to the slogan, "The
Jews are our misfortune." There was little outcry when
the Nazi's chanted, "Germany wake up, Judah drop
dead." There is no record of a serious protest to the
vicious words found in the SA *Sturmlied*: "and when
Jewish blood spurts from the knife, things will go twice
as well." On at least five occasions, Hitler said these
words, verbatim: "Today I will once more be a prophet.
If the international Jewish financiers inside and outside
Europe should again succeed in plunging the nations
into a world war, the result will be . . . the annihilation
of the Jewish race throughout Europe."

Levin has indicated an atmosphere of non-involve-
ment in German politics in the second quarter of this
century. "As democracy had been held in contempt as a
decadent, Western notion, the Germans of the Weimar
period developed no taste for citizen participation in
political life and consequently, gained no experience.
Politics generally was dismissed as hypocritical and

compromising and few men wanted to be sullied by it. Decisions were left to authorities while the people of the nation looked on passively" (pp. 22-23). Lest there be an erroneous impression given, however, we must not overlook the active role which German scholarship had in supporting Hitler. Dr. Jacob Robinson has a summary paragraph on this:

The role of German scholarship in the development of the idea of physical destruction of Jews as a method of a "solution of the Jewish question" should not be underestimated. Some highlights were Eugen Duehring's suggestion of such a solution in his popular volume *Die Judenfrage* (1881): the rejection of the idea of humanitarianism by German scholars and authors (e.g., Paul de Lagarde in his *Programm fuer die konservative Partei Preussens* (1884), reproduced in his *Deutsche Schriften* (1937), 423: "We have to break with the idea of humanity"): characterization of humanity as sheer silliness (*Humanitaetsduselei*), and the perversion, extension, and active application to human society of the Darwinian principle of natural selection in justification of the killing off (*ausmerzen*) of human beings deemed "inferior" by the "theorists."

It is strongly believed that protest, particularly by religious and intellectual groups, could have shaken Hitler's determination about Jews. There is evidence that this is true from the reaction to Hitler's euthanasia program which in two years killed some 50,000 sick persons, people who were judged insane, infirm or in some other way a burden to their families and their state. Some religious figures spoke out and wrote against the measures. As Levin has indicated, and others concur, "church protests continued and popular opposition mounted until Hitler had to discontinue the program" (p. 304). However, such a reaction was not in evidence over the increasingly harsh treatment of

German Jews. And so World War II began with people concerned about territory, about honor, about self purification. Historian Lucy S. Dawidowicz put another construction on the events and illustratively titled her book *The War Against the Jews 1933-1945.*

What kinds of things were Jews subject to before the Nazis and others implemented a plan of "Final Solution"? One statistic may give an idea. From 1932 to 1934 Jews in Germany had a suicide rate which was 50 percent higher than that of non-Jews. Concentration camps appeared in 1933; by the end of that year there were fifty. Harassment and beatings of Jews continued and grew in frequency and ferocity, culminating in *Crystal Night*, a brief period of organized terror (November 9-10, 1938) in which the destruction of 76 synagogues, 171 homes and 815 shops was reported by Reinhard Heydrich to Goering. Another 191 synagogues had been set on fire and 36 Jews were murdered. This organized, concerted effort also resulted in the arrest and incarceration of 20,000 Jews. On the day following, 680 Jews committed suicide.

Jewish children were tormented by other students as well as teachers and administrators in schools. Boycotts of Jewish businesses were effected. Jews had to be so identified on their passports. Expropriation of property and imprisonment—including the separation of families—became highly common. All of this, of course, led to the death camps, the camps about which so many people after the war claimed not to know existed. We may ask again, as we consider what went on there: Who designed them? Who built them? Who operated them? Who tortured and murdered them? Many who did these things called themselves Christians. What implication does this have for those of us who now call ourselves Christian?

What exactly went on in the death camps? Here is how Adolf Eichmann, the master killer from the "master race," describes an event in his career. He tells of seeing his first Jewish execution at Minsk:

I was sent by my immediate superior, General Muller.
. . . He liked to send me around on his behalf. I was in effect a traveling salesman for the Gestapo, just as I once had been a traveling salesman for an oil company in Austria.

Muller had heard that Jews were being shot near Minsk and wanted a report. . . . They had already started, so I could see only the finish. Although I was wearing a leather coat which reached almost to my ankles, it was very cold. I watched the last group of Jews undress, down to their shirts. They walked the last 100 or 200 yards—they were not driven—then they jumped into the pit. It was impressive to see them all jumping into the pit without offering any resistance whatsoever. Then the men of the squad banged away into the pit with their rifles and machine pistols.

Why did that scene linger so long in my memory? Perhaps because I had children myself. And there were children in that pit. I saw a woman hold a child of a year or two into the air, pleading. At that moment all I wanted to say was, "Don't shoot, hand over the child." Then the child was hit. I was so close that later I found bits of brains splattered on my long leather coat. My driver helped me remove them. Then we returned to Berlin.

(Levin, pp. 291-292.)

Here is the testimony of a Polish guard at Auschwitz, given at the Nuremberg trial:

WITNESS: . . . women carrying children were [always] sent with them to the crematorium. [Children were of no labor value so they were killed. The mothers were sent along, too, because separation might lead to panic, hysteria—which might slow up the destruction process,

HARRY JAMES CARGAS

and this could not be afforded. It was simpler to
condemn the mothers too and keep things quiet and
smooth.] The children were then torn from their parents
outside the crematorium and sent to the gas chambers
separately. [At that point, crowding more people into the
gas chambers became the most urgent consideration.
Separating meant that more children could be packed in
separately, or they could be thrown in over the heads of
adults once the chamber was packed.] When the
extermination of the Jews in the gas chambers was at its
height, orders were issued that children were to be
thrown straight into the crematorium furnaces, or into
pits near the crematorium, without being gassed first.

SMIRNOV (Russian prosecutor): How am I to understand this? Did they throw them into the fire alive, or did
they kill them first?

WITNESS: They threw them in alive. Their screams
could be heard at the camp. It is difficult to say how
many children were destroyed in this way.

SMIRNOV: Why did they do this?

WITNESS: It's very difficult to say. We don't know
whether they wanted to economize on gas, or if it was
because there was not enough room in the gas chambers.

Rudolf Hoess, the commander at Auschwitz, who
confessed that "I personally arranged the gassing of two
millions persons between June-July 1941 and the end of
1943," recalled this in his memoirs: "I remember, too, a
woman who tried to throw her children out of the gas
chamber, just as the door was closing. Weeping, she
called out: 'At least let my precious children live.' There
were many such scenes which affected all who witnessed them" (see *Commandant at Auschwitz*, New
York, 1961, pp. 140-141).

Next we may cite an account which, as one author
describes it, "froze the Nuremberg Court with pity and

horror."

On 5 October 1942, when I visited the building office at Subno, my foreman Hubert Moennikes . . . told me that in the vicinity of the site, Jews from Dubno had been shot in three large pits, each about 30 meters long and 3 meters deep. About 1,500 persons had been killed daily. All of the 5,000 Jews who had still been living in Dubno before the pogrom were to be liquidated. As the shootings had taken place in his presence he was still much upset.

Thereupon I drove to the site, accompanied by Moennikes and saw near it great mounds of earth, about 30 meters long and 2 meters high. Several trucks stood in front of the mounds. Armed Ukranian militia drove the people off the trucks under the supervision of an S.S. man. The militia men acted as guards on the trucks and drove them to and from the pit. All these people had the regulation yellow patches on the front and back of their clothes, and thus could be recognized as Jews.

Moennikes and I went directly to the pits. Nobody bothered us. Now I heard rifle shots in quick succession, from behind one of the earth mounds. The people who had got off the trucks—men, women and children of all ages—had to undress upon the order of an S.S. man who carried a riding or dog whip. They had to put down their clothes in fixed places, sorted according to shoes, top clothing, and underclothing. I saw a heap of shoes of about 800 to 1,000 pairs, great piles of under-linen and clothing. Without screaming or weeping these people undressed, stood around in family groups, kissed each other, said farewells and waited for a sign from another S.S. man, who stood near the pit, also with a whip in his hand.

During the fifteen minutes that I stood near the pit, I heard no complaint or plea for mercy. I watched a family of about 8 persons, a man and woman, both about 50, with their children of about 1, 8, and 10, and two grown-up daughters of about 20 to 24. An old woman with snow-white hair was holding the one-year old child and singing to it and tickling it. The child was cooing with delight. The couple were looking on with tears in their eyes. The father was holding the hand of a boy of about 10 years old and speaking to him softly; the boy was fighting his tears. The father pointed toward the sky, stroked his head, and seemed to explain something to him. At that moment the S.S. man at the pit shouted something to his comrade. The latter counted off about 20 persons and instructed them to go behind the earth mound. Among them was the family which I have mentioned.

I well remember a girl, slim and with black hair, who, as she passed close to me, pointed to herself and said, "Twenty-three!" I walked around the mound, and found myself confronted by a tremendous grave. People were closely wedged together and lying on top of each other so that only their heads were visible. Nearly all had blood running over their shoulders from their heads. Some of the people shot were still moving. Some were lifting their arms and turning their heads to show that they were still alive. The pit was already two-thirds full. I estimated that it already contained about a thousand people.

I looked for the man who did the shooting. He was an S.S. man, who sat at the edge of the narrow end of the pit, his feet dangling into the pit. He had a tommy gun on his knees and he was smoking a cigarette. The people, completely naked, went down some steps which were cut in the clay wall of the pit and clambered over the heads of the people lying there, to the place where the S.S. man directed them. They lay down in front of the dead or injured people; some caressed those who were still alive and spoke to them in a low voice. Then I heard a series of shots.

I looked into the pit and saw that the bodies were twitching or the heads lying already motionless on top of the bodies that lay before them. Blood was running from their necks. I was surprised that I was not ordered away, but I saw that there were two or three postmen in uniform nearby. The next batch was approaching already. They went down into the pit, lined themselves up against the previous victims and were shot. When I walked back, around the mound. I noticed another truckload of people which had just arrived. This time it included sick and infirm people. An old, very thin woman with terribly thin legs was undressed by others who were already naked, while two people held her up. The woman appeared to be paralyzed. The naked people carried the woman around the mound. I left with Moennikes and drove in my car back to Dubno.

On the morning of the next day when I again visited the site, I saw about 30 naked people lying near the pit—about 30 to 50 meters away from it. Some of them were still alive; they looked straight in front of them with a fixed stare and seemed to notice neither the chilliness of the morning nor the workers of my firm who stood around. A girl of about 20 spoke to me and asked me to give her clothes and help her escape. At that moment we heard a fast car approach and I noticed that it was an S.S. detail. I moved away to my site. Then minutes later we heard shots from the vicinity of the pit. The Jews still alive had been ordered to throw the corpses into the pit—then they themselves had to lie down in this to be shot in the neck.

(Levin, pp. 264-266.)

Here is a letter from a man who escaped death and wrote to warn other Jews about what was happening:

My very dear friends,

I did not answer you until now, because I knew nothing very definite about all the things I've been told. Alas, to our great misfortune, we now know everything! I had here at my home an eyewitness who was saved by the grace of heaven. . . . I found out everything from him. The place where they are exterminated is called

Chelmno, near Dabia, and they are buried in the neighboring forest of Lachow. The men are killed in two ways: shooting or gas. . . . For several days they have been taking thousands of Jews from Lodz and have done the same to them. Don't imagine that all this is written by a madman. Alas, it is the terrible tragic truth. . . . "Man, rend thy clothing, put on sackcloth with ashes, and go out into the midst of the city, and cry out with a loud and bitter cry." I am so tired that my pen can write no more. Creator of the universe, help us!

> (Levin, p. 306.)

But the man was not believed. His friends could not accept the truth of what some human beings were doing to other human beings.

Let one more narration suffice. In Warsaw, on August 12, 1942, an orphanage for Jewish children was "evacuated." The founder and director was Janusz Korczak, a physician, writer and educator. As a medical doctor he could have remained in the Warsaw Ghetto for some time longer, but he chose to accompany his children on the deportation. An eyewitness describes the scene:

And so a long line is formed in the front of the orphanage on Slisks Street. A long procession, children, small, tiny, rather precocious, emaciated, weak, shriveled and shrunk. They carry shabby packages, some have schoolbooks, notebooks under their arms. No one is crying.

Slowly they go down the steps, line up in rows, in perfect order and discipline, as usual. Their little eyes are turned towards the doctor. They are strangely calm; they feel almost well. The doctor is going with them, so what do they have to be afraid of? They are not alone, they are not abandoned.

Dr. Korczak busies himself with the children with a sober earnestness. He buttons the coat of one child, ties up a package of another, or straightens the cap of a third. Then he wipes off a tear which is rolling down the thin little face of a child.

Then the processing starts out. It is starting out for a trip from which—everybody feels it—one never comes back. All these young, budding lives. . . . And all this is marching quietly and orderly to the place of their untimely doom. The children are calm, but inwardly they must feel it, they must sense it intuitively. Otherwise how could you explain the deadly seriousness on their pale little faces? But they are marching quietly in orderly rows, calm and earnest, and at the head of them is Janusz Korczak.

(Levin, p. 326.)

Must we go on? Can we go on? How can we? And yet we must. Else the next holocaust may await all of us, the one which will consume the earth.

Who were the people who devised the policies which Christians and others carried out? Adolf Hitler was a baptized Catholic who claimed to be doing God's work in killing Jews. Paul Joseph Goebbels, propaganda expert, came from a strict Catholic family and had his education, in part, funded by the Albertus Magnus Society. Auschwitz's Commandant Rudolf Hoess said he took his Catholic religion "very seriously." Heinrich Himmler, the ruthless head of the SS was from a devout Catholic family. Reinhard Heydrich, who led the Reich Security Service, was Catholic. It has not gone unremarked that Hitler's heir apparent, Hermann Goering was given the full funeral rites of the Lutheran church.

We must not leave the impression that these men were followed blindly by all Europeans, or even that all remained indifferent. Gordon Zahn has told us the story of Franz Jagersdatter, the Austrian peasant who disobeyed his priest and his bishop and was martyred for refusing to fight in the German army. Protestant theologian Dietrich Bonhoeffer's resistance and death are also well documented. And there are, perhaps, several thousand more. The man who was to be Pope John XXIII, when Apostolic Delegate to Turkey, aided Hungarian Jews to escape. The head of the Orthodox Church in Rumania, Patriarch Nikodemus, courageously denounced the persecutions and thus no doubt saved the lives of thousands of Jews. Bulgaria's Metropolitan Stephan insisted that God alone could determine the fate of the Jews and that men had no authority to persecute them and led resistance in his country. Italians did not cooperate with Hitler's Jewish policies. A French Capuchin, Father Marie-Benoit, helped organize a false document mill, including certificates of baptism, to help Jews escape. Railway workers in Belgium earned honor in helping Jews on transport trains to escape the crematoria by refusing to lock the railway car doors. Nora Levin reports that "20,000 Dutch Christians were deported to concentration camps because they opposed Nazi racial decrees, many of them first to Buchenwald, where they were slowly tortured, then to Mathausen in Austria" (Levin, p. 409). Of 2,000 Jews in Finland, only four were deported. We can imagine the resistance to the anti-Jewish policies there. In Galacia, Metropolitan Andreas Szeptycki, Archbishop of Lvov who headed the Ukrainian Greek Catholic Church, refused to allow religious service of any kind to Ukrainians who killed Jews. This half-paralyzed, seventy-seven year old man personally hid Jews in his quarters and ordered nuns in convents to do likewise.

The story of Danish non-cooperation is probably best known around the world. It is said that when Jews in Denmark were ordered to wear the Star of David as an emblem of humiliation, King Christian X followed by the rest of the citizens, did likewise. The tale is not literally true, but it does have symbolic veracity. It seems that nearly all Danes, including their monarch, were extremely supportive of their co-citizens, the Jewish Danes. There were some 7,000 Jews in Denmark, and 474 were caught by the Gestapo and sent to concentration camps. The majority were rescued and spent the remainder of the war years as free persons in neutral Sweden.

The Danes were motivated by an admirable sense of individual responsibility. Jorgan Barford, who was President of the Association of Danish Prisoners from the Fight for Freedom, tells this story:

> The German Plenipotentiary in Denmark, Dr. Werner Best, raised the matter of an action against the Jews with his superiors in Berlin on September 8th, 1943. Best happened to mention this to the German shipping expert in Denmark, G.F. Duckwitz, who was an opponent of the Nazis' terror methods and who had made contact with some Danish Social Democrat politicians, H. Hedtoft-Hansen and H. C. Hansen. Duckwitz was furious and even went to Berlin to prevent this manhunt from being put into effect, and later went to Stockholm for the same purpose. However, by the 28th of September he had to admit that he was powerless, and as he by then knew the date when the persecution of the Jews was to begin, he passed on this information to the above-mentioned Danish politicians.
>
> *Escape from Nazi Terror* (Copenhagen, 1968), p. 11.

The politicians then warned the head of the Jewish community, High Court Advocate C.B. Henriques, and the message was communicated to nearly every Jew in the country. When the Germans came to arrest Jews, very few were at home, many being given refuge by Christian friends. In addition to this, Bishop H. Fuglsang Damgaard, wrote this pastoral letter, to be read in churches throughout the country—written on behalf of all Danish bishops (in 1943):

The Danish bishops have on September 29th, this year, forwarded the following communication to the leading German authorities through the heads of the government departments:

Wherever Jews are persecuted as such on racial or religious grounds the Christian Church is in duty bound to protest against this action:

1. Because we can never forget that the Lord of the Christian Church, Jesus Christ, was born in Bethlehem of the Virgin Mary according to God's promise to His Chosen People, Israel. The history of the Jewish people before the birth of Jesus contains the preparation for the salvation God has prepared for all mankind in Christ. This is shown by the fact that the Old Testament is a part of our Bible.

2. Because persecution of the Jews conflicts with that recognition and love of man that are a consequence of the gospel which the church of Jesus Christ was founded to preach. Christ is no respecter of persons, and He has taught us to see that every human life is precious in the eyes of God. Gal. 3, 28.

3. Because it conflicts with the concept of justice which prevails in the Danish people, settled in our Danish Christian culture for centuries. In consequence of this, equal rights and responsibility before the law, and freedom of religion, are secured to all Danish citizens according to the words of the constitution.

We regard religious freedom as the right to worship God according to vocation and conscience and hence that neither race nor religion can, of themselves, deprive any citizen of rights, liberty or property. Despite differences of religious opinion, we will struggle for the right of our Jewish brothers and sisters to preserve the same liberty that we prize more highly than life itself.

The leaders of the Danish Church are fully aware of our duty to be law-abiding citizens, who do not set themselves up against those exercising authority over us, but at the same time we are in conscience bound to assert the law and to protest against any violation of it. Therefore we shall, if occasion should arise, unequivocally acknowledge the words that we should obey God rather than Man.

(Barford, pp. 12-14.)

The rest is inspiring history. The smuggling of Jews into Sweden took a widely coordinated and extremely secret effort. Many persons risked their freedom and their lives in this defiance of the Nazis. (The role of Swedish citizens must also be commended. There was not as much personal risk involved, certainly, but the Swedes didn't merely accept the new immigrants. They trained them in the language, found them jobs and places to live and obviously did risk infuriating German authorities whose war plans always proved capricious enough so that even neutral Sweden had to be wary.)

But such a story is, unhappily, unique. Other Christians were not so helpful. For example, the Vatican was asked by the Vichy government in France about the law of June 2, 1941 which isolated Jews and deprived them of their rights. The response was direct. "In principle, there is nothing in these measures which the Holy See would find to criticize" (Fleischner, p. 12). There is even evidence to lead one to conclude, as Nora Levin has, that early in the war, at least, "the Vatican expressed its interest in a German victory" (p. 685). Later, there were perhaps other reasons for Rome's inaction. "When Dr. Eduardo Senatro, the Berlin correspondent of *L'Osservatore Romano*, asked him whether he would not protest the exterminations, the Pope [Pius XII] is reported to have answered, 'Dear friend, do not forget that millions of Catholics serve in the German armies. Shall I bring them into conflicts of conscience?' " (Levin, p. 691).

Alas, Pius was not alone in his silence. Even the U.S., with its large Jewish population, did comparatively little. And Great Britain, with Anthony Eden as a great stumbling block to Jewish rescue efforts, almost actively persecuted Jews trying to escape Hitler. No one knew what was happening? Henry Morgenthau, Jr., Secretary of Treasury in the United States, gives the lie to this:

> We knew in Washington, from August 1942 on, that the Nazis were planning to exterminate all the Jews of Europe. Yet, for nearly 18 months after the first reports of the Nazi horror plan, the State Department did practically nothing. Officials dodged their grim responsibility, procrastinated when concrete rescue schemes were placed before them, and even suppressed information about atrocities in order to prevent an outraged public opinion from forcing their hand. . . . The Treasury's responsibility for licensing monetary transactions abroad meant that we had to pass on the financial phases of refugee relief plans. This gave us a front-row view of those 18 terrible months of inefficiency, buck-passing, bureaucratic delay and sometimes what appeared to be calculated obstructionism. . . . Cautious action. . . . Lacking either the administrative drive or the emotional commitment, they could not bring about prompt United States action on behalf of the desperate people.
>
> (Levin, p. 669.)

So the annihilations went on, with impunity, as it were. Heinrich Himmler, who insisted that members of the SS must believe in God, could thus, unchallenged by serious moral attacks, speak of the honor and decency of the work of slaughter. "By and large, however, we can say that we have performed this task in love of our people. And we have suffered no damage from it in our inner self, in our soul, in our character" (Fleischner, p. 38). How smug. And there was no significant challenge.

Not even after the terrible events of 1939-1945 was there a moral cry of pain from certain quarters. Goering was buried with full funeral rites of the Lutheran church, as noted. Until recently, a mass was celebrated annually in Madrid for Hitler (though not for the victims) and it has not been lost on investigators that, at the war's close, the Vatican and others close to it helped thousands of war criminals to escape, including Franz Stangl, the commandant of Treblinka. There is more, ". . . in 1948, the German Evangelical Conference at Darmstadt, meeting in the country which had only recently carried out this genocide, proclaimed that the terrible Jewish suffering in the Holocaust was a divine visitation and a call to the Jews to cease their rejection and ongoing crucifixion of Christ" (Fleischner, pp. 12-13). As Irving Greenberg has asked, "May one morally be a Christian after this?" It is, I believe, the question which obsesses me. Was Christianity in some way buried at Auschwitz? If so, is a resurrection of a more humanly significant Christianity, less dedicated to its own preservation than to the teachings of Christ, not so fixed on the next world that it is incapable of interacting with this world, now, is such a resurrection taking place in us, in me? That is the motivation for my words. What I have written here only hints at a response to the question. The meaningful answers will come from lives, not books or talks.

III
THE EVIDENCE

How does one approach a subject of such moral and emotional magnitude as this study of atrocity photography of the Holocaust? And yet, once the subject became visible, how could it be ignored? My obsession with the Holocaust as the greatest Christian tragedy since the crucifixion of Jesus is long standing. I want to explore its significance for myself as a professing Christian, to insist that each post-Holocaust Christian must also approach this overwhelming subject if her or his Christianity is to be meaningful and to show survivors of that catastrophe (and that means every person on earth in one way or another) that we Christians are sincere in our examination of what occurred in a Christian—though not a Christ-centered—civilization. The Holocaust is a failure in Christian history. Is Christianity dead? If so, I must know it. If it lives, how is this so, and how is my own religious commitment affected?

Who am I to take up questions of such magnitude? Nobody special. I don't feel that I am doing anything that many others cannot do better. My only response is that I *am* doing research and writing on the Holocaust where enough others are not.

A necessary observation: There are a number of volumes out now professing to prove that the Holocaust never really happened, that events of that Crime as we know them were invented by Zionists eager to gain sympathy for their plan for the establishment of the state of Israel after World War II. Nobody who has read any of these works can ever approach Holocaust studies without the presence of such revisionist history in mind. We may pity authors who spend so much energy dedicated to shame. And we must prove where they are wrong. The book you hold now is one such proof. The eyes of survivors are another. To spit on the graves of the Holocaust dead is indeed to give the Nazi cause continued support.

The photographs in this volume were acquired at Yad Vashem Holocaust Memorial Center in Jerusalem. In the archives there are some 40,000 photos of which these few are representatives. I had planned to spend three weeks on the project. After two weeks, having gone through about 10,000 photographs, I abruptly left Israel. The research had such an overwhelming impact on me that I had to come home to kiss my wife and hug my children.

Ovens for human beings. Are these the symbol of our century? The fact that someone even thought of them is staggering enough. Many others, of course, had to approve of them: committees, officials, the very highest Nazis. Their designers would have to be approached. "Will you blueprint ovens for us so that we can dispose of Jewish bodies? This will help us free Europe of a pestilence and it will leave no trace of what we did." Could the reply have been, "It will be an honor to serve the Reich"? Next there are the contractors. Was there competitive bidding for the job of constructing these furnaces? Were government officials bribed so that certain companies might gain advantage over others? How much profit was made by the people who helped in this way to carry out the final solution to the Jewish problem? This photograph is of ovens at Dachau. The three men who are placing the body into the crude crematorium are called *Sonderkommandos*. They are themselves prisoners whose job is to dispose of other prisoners. Usually, a *Sonderkommando* worked about three months at his job, then he himself became a victim of the ovens. This seems to be clearly a public relations photograph of some kind. A special effort is being made here to tell someone something. Otherwise, given all we know of camp efficiency, all of the ovens would have been operating at once. How else could up to 9,000 bodies a day be disposed of? Did the photographer have anything to say to the workers? Did he balance them off for aesthetic purposes? Did he have to make certain that each was so positioned that the body was in no way blocked from view? What are the *Sonderkommandos* thinking as they are being forced to pose? Has their work destroyed their sensibilities? Are they totally beyond caring? Note the lack of other men, the neatness of the area where we might expect grim filth. Public relations photograph indeed.

How old is the bottom figure in this photograph? Perhaps seven. But his eyes contain centuries. What a pitiful incongruity. Innocence, by its very nature, does not encompass experience. But then this photograph is of a situation which is not consistent with nature. The Holocaust was, by every civilized measure, anti-natural. The boy intuits this. Something is horribly topsy-turvy, terribly frightening. A man is holding a weapon on him, during this roundup of Jews in Warsaw. For what reason? No reason could ever be invented to justify what is happening in this scene and the real cause is ludicrous in the root sense of that word. This boy is being taken to his death because he has been judged a danger to European equilibrium. He is a Jew. That is crime enough in some people's minds. And while we could focus our attention exclusively on him in this picture, there are others who need to be considered. For instance, the child with his hands raised isn't even the youngest Pole in the group. Just above his right shoulder we see another who is about four or five years old. Another threat, another Christ-killer to some. Another boy to the left of center, looking off to his right, also exhibits in his eyes a terror no child should know. Eyes, in fact, can be considered a theme, if we dare to be academic about this setting. The camera's eye must be considered. It *must* be. Who has dared to take this photograph? For what

66

purpose? Why memorialize this sin? What is the intended audience? Who will enjoy viewing this? Clearly this picture could not have been made with official permission. The victims were not snapping shutters. No, the persecutors were. Note that no eyes of the prisoners are looking at the camera. Those eyes are concentrated on something other than publicity. There is one, however, who is looking directly into the lens: the guard who has his gun directed at the little boy up front. We may take it that he is posing for this photographer. Why? Is he proud of what he is doing? Is he pleased to be carrying out his government's policy concerning Jews? Did he request a copy of the photo to show his friends and family? I have heard that after this photograph became famous, this guard was found as a civilian. I do not know the accuracy of this, but if true, he really has seen *himself* in this situation. How does he feel about it? Does he ever wonder if God's eye has recorded the same event? Does he have some thoughts about Judgment Day? What else did he do in the war that is memorable?

What unlimited power individual soldiers had. Nobody could stop their outrageous behavior. In fact some wished to record human abuse in order to enjoy it later as the photographer of this snap apparently did. The woman on the left is physically very beautiful. But she is not proud of her body at the instant recorded here. We can only imagine what comments the soldiers are making about her nakedness. Perhaps the photographer joined in the merriment. It is possible, even likely, that the picture taker is another soldier who joins the others in taking turns at humiliating prisoners. "Next time you take *my* photo," he may have said. And we wonder, "Why the photography?" The woman's body language is so pitiably obvious. Her somewhat stooped shoulders indicate her inward attitude. The set mouth, the downcast eyes all contribute to her personal "atmosphere" if we may say that. What was she before the war? A teacher, a secretary? Perhaps a student. No doubt somebody's sister, a daughter and a granddaughter. A neighbor too, the friend of many and possibly a fiancee. She may even have been married. (There is no ring on her finger but Germans appropriated such things almost immediately.) Did she have children? There is no question that some of the people with whom she had normal human relationships probably saw this moment. The woman on the right, who shared it, may have been her sister or her friend. What happened after the photo was snapped? Did the Nazis touch these women? Did they make them walk the street nude, dance for them, howl like dogs? Nazis did it with others, we know. Were these soldiers braggarts about their contributions to the war efforts of the Third Reich? Did they tell about their heroic behavior on occasions like this?

It is difficult to think of the men looking out through the barbed wire as in any way fortunate and yet, relatively speaking, they are. The reason is because they are near some ventilation on the train car into which they have been crammed. If their ride is typical of the experience of so many others, this access to air may save their lives. Other women and men have ridden for four days without food or water to their destruction camp. Some experienced 100° heat—others freezing temperatures. Many did not survive. Others went insane. A host saw relatives and friends, babies and the very old, die during the trip. The majority of these deaths, we learn, were agonizing for those who perished and for the helpless who watched as well. People befouled themselves. Washing facilities were, of course, non-existent. On many of the freight cars sleeping space—that is, room in which to lie down—was also non-existent. Fights broke out among prisoners who, in their frustrations, turned on each other the anger which was really meant for their captors. Corpses on the trains caused disease since some persons died within minutes after having been herded onto the prison on wheels. Who were the railroad engineers who carried the human cargo to camps of destruction? Who were the laborers who locked tightly the handles on the freight cars (as seen in this photograph) which assured the Nazis that their quarry would arrive at journey's end? (There was a number of Dutch railroad workers who saw to it that, when the Nazi troops left after supervising the boarding of the trains, the handles on the freight cars were mysteriously opened again.) And what of the many citizens who watched the cattle cars go by, load after load after load, without pity or protest? We condemn them. But if we were in their positions would we . . . ?

The legend etched in Hebrew beside this heap of human bones says this: "Among the transgressions of the Germans." A pile of broken skeletons, saved from becoming fertilizer by the conquering Allied forces. For some reason the skulls at the lower left have been arranged in a rather orderly fashion as opposed to the random mass of other bones in this pyramid of infamy. Perhaps the skulls were to be used for some sort of medical experimentation—the kind that we know took place through which the Nazis were trying to prove, by measurements, the inferiority of Jews, Gypsies and certain others. Or possibly the skulls were so displayed by zealous liberators

who wanted to be sure that the full impact of this scene would register in the minds and hearts of us, the viewers. As if we wouldn't be horrified enough without such preparations! How long were prisoners subject to viewing scenes like this one, even while they could hear the guns of British, Russian or American forces coming ever closer to that long hoped for yet seemingly impossible moment when the barbed wire seen here could be torn down and people could once again resume the tradition of being people? The legend, "Among the transgressions of the Germans" is so succinct, so telling, so properly understood. Anyone could be practically emotionally destroyed by such atrocities. Do we become immune to them, at some level of saturation? Are we in danger of identifying with one American journalist who immortalized herself on a radio talk show by responding to something another guest had said by saying, *Oh, here we go with those 6,000,000 again?* She was disgusted that anyone would want to keep remembering the Holocaust, its victims and its implications.

71

In the emotional disorienting world of the concentration camp universe, we cannot be certain that the death of this man was met with sadness by all of the prisoners. Some may have stood to gain from his death. Perhaps he left behind a decent pair of boots or a precious spoon. Maybe he had a preferred sleeping place that one of the other men can now acquire. It is possible that this man was in such a weakened condition that another had to work extra hard to cover for him, and so the stronger man will feel relieved when he knows that his burden has been temporarily lightened. Under normal circumstances we would criticize such opportunism as selfish, morally, reprehensible. But we do not here consider normal times. We may dare to suggest that while the letter of certain moral codes was violated, sin among most victims at Auschwitz did not take place. Lying is wrong, but for a twelve year old boy to say he is sixteen, so that he might be allowed to live as a laborer rather than perish as a child, is not to do wrong. Stealing is regarded as a fault, but for a prisoner to smuggle an extra bowl of soup, or a pair of socks off a dead body, is to commit no fault. To fail to love one's neighbor as one's self—in this case one's neighbor being one's guard, one's captor, one's tormentor—is not to morally fail at all. When we learn of some prisoners killing Nazis, changing sexual preferences, committing suicide—all traditional taboos in our culture—dare we accuse these men and women of anything? What of women or boys who prostituted themselves to survive? How easy it would be to turn on them and point a superior finger. But anyone who would do so would be one who had not undergone similar pressures. And it would be deflecting the aim of where the finger should be pointing— towards the perpetrators of the Holocaust rather than the victims.

73

HARRY JAMES CARGAS

How proud can one be of the work one does? Not only so proud as to document it via camera, but also proud enough to use it as the picture side of a postcard. That's right, this snapshot was made into a postcard! That implies that the men in this picture were going to send a lot of messages to a lot of friends, bragging about their contributions to the cause of the Third Reich. Look, pals, here's what we do in the army. There I am, second from the right, doing my part to make the world rid of Jews. It is even possible that one or several of the living in this photograph did not participate in the hangings but got into the scene so that they might appear to be "heroes" anyway. The soldier on the left seems a bit camera shy; his eyes are averted perhaps because he is nervous before the lens. Not nervous, mind you, because bodies which he helped to hang, are dangling behind him. Just a little unsure in front of the photographer—like most of us. His smile lets us know what he thinks about his work. Possibly he sent this postcard to his mother. Maybe she would show it with pride to other family members, to neighbors, to friends, at the butcher shop.

The facilities for execution here are not the most modern, or even remotely efficient. Thus the victims probably died long, agonizing deaths. Anyone who could grin the way these troops are doing could easily have tormented those about to be murdered; might readily have enjoyed watching them dangle and gasp for breath. The scene is an isolated one so nobody could see what was going on. The killers had great freedom. On the other hand, since no one could see, why not take a photo, else they couldn't brag.

All soldiers remember target practice during their days as new recruits in the military. There were all the jokes about someday that bullseye turning into the hated enemy. No doubt that enemy was conceived as another soldier, one who posed some threat in return. Danger—there is the vocation of the man in uniform. It is seen as honorable to risk one's life to defend national ideals. How ironic all that rhetoric is when applied to what the rifleman in this photograph is about to do. He is almost a model for marksmanship trainees. True, his right elbow is probably a little lower than most instructors would like, but his left hand grips the weapon properly and his stance, with feet spread apart for good balance, is certainly correct. Most everything is "right" except the target. An unarmed father, it appears, is shielding his child from the inevitable which is just a few feet from the back of his head. We can imagine the kind of gaping wound that will result from such close range shooting. We wish to ask this Nazi the questions we want answered by so many others: "How do you justify what you did here?" "How many times did you commit such atrocities?" "Did you welcome such assignments?" (After all, these were the safer duties; far back from the front lines, with unarmed and dispirited victims.) And the father, what was going on in his mind? Certainly there was no hope for him or the child. Perhaps his only prayer was for swift death for both of them. That is not the kind of prayer that most of us have for our children. It is an unnatural prayer, bred by an unnatural time. No doubt the child had more hope unless the child had seen others gunned down in similar fashion seconds and minutes and hours and days before.

Nobody could accuse the Germans of not having a sense of humor. The entrance to Auschwitz is bridged by the words, "Work makes one free." That's the kind of slogan we might expect in a Charlie Chaplin film where a greedy business mogul is actually trying to enslave his employees in order to increase production. The use of the word "free" in connection with the camp inmates is scandalously ironic. Over another camp prisoners who entered read the words, "Homeland of the Jews." This was in mockery of Zionists whose aspiration was to re-establish Israel (which at that time was not a political entity) so that those Jews who wished might have a country in which they could feel they truly belonged. If by

"homeland" is meant not only the place where one finds one's roots but also the site where one dies, then that word was truly used. More honest, more appropriate words, are now found on a plaque in the infamous camp of Dachau. They are by the American philosopher George Santayana who wrote that "Those who forget the past are condemned to repeat it." The wisdom of this statement is what spurs certain people to keep the memory of the Holocaust alive. There is no attempt here to wallow in the inhuman events of that great tragedy. Rather there is the hope (and "hope" is a term not usually associated with the Holocaust) that perhaps, by recalling what happened before and during the Nazi regime, we can prevent similar crimes from occurring. A Russian proverb puts it even more bluntly than Santayana, and Aleksandr Solzhenitzyn uses it to begin his *Gulag Archipelago*: "Forget the past and you'll lose both your eyes." The past, all of it, is our heritage. Either we learn from it or we shall not. Either we shall prepare for new holocausts for our children and granchildren or we shall not.

Initially, one could mistake what is going on in this scene. A group of children, walking in an orderly fashion, to get on some trucks. Perhaps going to a picnic, a zoo outing, a museum visit. Why not, that's what children do. But the situation here is grotesquely different. These children are enemies of the Third Reich, the thousand year empire which Adolf Hitler is constructing. They are Jews as can be seen by the stars of David on the backs of a number of coats. As Jews, their blood threatens Aryan blood and therefore must commingle only with the earth, not with other blood. Scholars indicate that of the approximately 6,000,000 Jews who perished at the will of the Nazis and their collaborators, about a million were under the age of twelve. As we think of the terror, the loneliness, the sense of abandonment, perhaps of betrayal by their parents, which each child experienced, we can feel only shame at what certain human beings were able to conceive, let alone execute. One boy seems to be dressed in a sailor suit. When his mother bought it for him, did he put it on proudly, looking forward to the day when he would be in his nation's navy, wearing an official uniform? Most boys have such dreams. What was he thinking about when the photograph was taken—something less pleasant we can be sure. Four adults can be distinguished in this picture, all grim faced, no doubt because they *know*. The woman at the left of the column has her yellow star displayed. How does she feel as she tries to comfort the youngsters, perhaps telling them soft lies about where they are going, trying not to terrorize them because how can they understand? But how could anyone understand, then or now?

Synagogue scrolls are sacred to Jews. Here they appear to be in some danger and these men are trying to protect them. Judging by the condition of the wall and other things in this scene, we may be viewing a badly desecrated temple, one which was perhaps razed by the Nazis. The care with which the two men regard the scrolls tells much about the Jewish situation. One man is so pained that he appears to be crying in a kind of tearless agony. The second man looks very concernedly, rather gently at the holy documents which he carries. Probably the pair is being forced to turn over the religious artifacts to the enemies of the Jews. We can infer this from the fact of the photograph having been taken. It is doubtful if a Jewish person would have attempted to immortalize this moment. It is more likely that we are witnessing the instant before the parchments themselves will be destroyed. It was part of the Nazi program not only to kill Jews but to humiliate them as well. Raul Hilberg, in his comprehensive volume on *The Destruction of European Jews*, writes of three historical policies against his people in Western Europe. For about four centuries after the birth of Christ there was a policy of attempted conversion of the Jews to Christianity. As that proved less than overwhelmingly successful, a policy of expulsion was adopted. Finally, in our time, came the ultimate technique of annihilation. However, somehow, murdering the Jews didn't seem to be enough. First they had to be robbed of their humanity. They were numbered, shaved to nakedness, dressed in deliberately ill fitting clothing, beaten and starved and otherwise tortured. Only *then* were they killed. Knowing this, we can see that the religion of the Jews could not be spared. This by people who called themselves Christians; who spoke of Hebrew scriptures as their Old Testament!

Just an ordinary chimney, rising upward to float its discharge of ashes high above the community in which it is located. But because of chimneys like this at the crematorium at Mathausen, some Jews regard the clouds in the sky as symbols of dead relatives. We don't know how many bodies were reduced up this chimney, and it is almost blasphemous to speculate. If it had been just one body, that would be truly horrible. But what if the reality is closer to a quarter of a million? Or many more? The imagination is numbed by this possibility. The age of mass production became the time of mass destruction. The techniques of tremendous efficiency developed by industry were perverted for demonic uses. Jews have a religious obligation to pray *Kaddish* at the grave sites of their loved ones. Six million dead Jews either have no identifiable graves (countless having been interred in huge burial pits, often crunched in by bulldozers) or have no graves period—their ashes were simply scattered from the orifices of giant chimneys which frequently did their work non-stop, day and night, for long periods of time. Some crematoria were capable of disposing of 12,000 bodies a day. And no rabbi or descendant can pray near the remains of these people. Perhaps it is more accurate to say that the remains of the victims actually are near us all of the time. They are practically ubiquitous just as the crimes which exterminated them were all-encompassing in their evil. It may border on the overly sentimental to think of clouds representing people, or stars symbolizing the eyes of the dead children of the Holocaust. And yet . . .

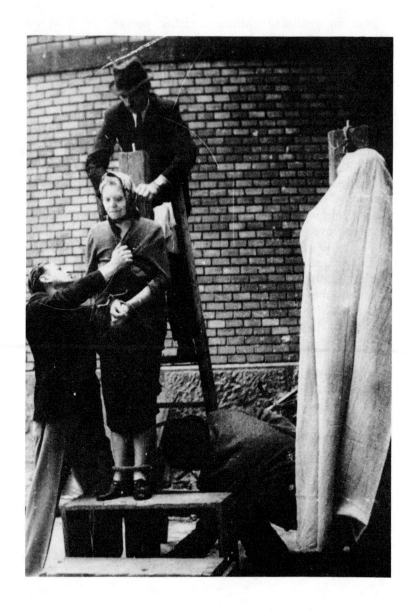

Such care is being taken to hang this woman properly. Look at the expressions of each of these men. They are paying such close attention to every last detail. They perform rather artistically for the photographer here, each relating so intently to a particular aspect of the unholy task literally *at hand(s)*! Note how well dressed the men are. The executioner on the left wears trousers that have been carefully creased. (This was long before the invention of perma-press.) And how about the man working from above, with tie and hat. When he left home, did his neighbors think that he was heading for the office? Did he ask his wife, "What's for dinner tonight?" thinking that today's work would not interfere with a hearty appetite? But we cannot only consider the killers. Our eyes are continually brought back to the woman who is soon to die. She seems hardly to pose a threat. She looks like my grandmother, is undoubtedly somebody's grandmother. What is she thinking? Is she praying? How frightened is this woman? Does she hope for some miracle to save her, or does she despair because she knows that a tremendous human slaughter is taking place, that she is only a single unit in an overwhelming event that will number 50,000,000 units? She may be almost at peace; somehow the camera suggests this. How many has she seen hanged before her? The corpse on the right suggests that there may have been several. How long will she be able to maintain a certain dignity, before the bulk of her body, in opposition to her neck, will force her to attempt to flail her legs and arms in some futile gesture toward life? Did she know the shrouded victim? Was it her husband or a child of hers? Did she die quickly?

A camp orchestra—there's a touch. Many Jewish artists, among them outstanding musicians, would "naturally" be incarcerated if all Jews were arrested. So these talented people could be made to perform. Either that or they would die immediately. Some call that a choice. We learn from Josef Bor in *The Terezin Requiem* and from Fania Fenelon (herself a member of a woman's orchestra at Birkenau, the extermination camp) in *Playing for Time* that programs were conducted for the entertainment of Adolf Eichmann, Heinrich Himmler and SS officials whenever it was convenient—for the Nazis. We can only speculate on whether or not the authorities got *extra* pleasure from concerts which were performed by people who had been degraded, lost everything, were starving and were subject to extermination. Did Himmler ever regret the fact that a particular outstanding soloist was not going to be thrilling audiences for much longer? Did Eichmann, after enjoying a symphony played by prisoners, ever have some doubts about the inferiority, the subhumanity of all Jews? Camp orchestras, we know, were forced to play at certain occasions when other inmates were entering gas chambers. The impact on the musicians themselves must have been curious. No doubt some thanked their parents for having started them off musically. Perhaps others were horrified because they found themselves hoping that other good players would die off so that the competition—literally for their very lives—would become less intense. What if a so-so cellist learns that a first rate cellist has just been transferred into the same camp? The newcomer may unwittingly become the enemy of the less accomplished performer. The *real* enemy, the Nazis, may well be overlooked under these incredible conditions. And Nazi music lovers enjoyed!

This is an extremely puzzling photograph. The expressions on the faces of the living in this Warsaw scene are almost as mystifying as the faces of the dead are horrifying. There seems to be some apprehension among the men standing; the rather self-conscious ear scratch by the individual on the right, accompanied by the nervous smile, indicates that. Yet not all of the four faces of the living that we can see appear to reflect abhorrence at the task to which they have been assigned. One man in the background has dropped his head, hidden himself mainly, perhaps out of shame—not that he can be deemed guilty of any immoral act, but possibly he experienced shame that humanity could come to this. Are the workers, Jews if we are to judge from the one right sleeve which is visible, so jaded by their work that they are no longer revulsed by what they do? If that is so, how do they treat the bodies in the act of burial—with utter disrespect? Does one of these men whisper a prayer for the souls departed from these bodies, since surely no rabbi will be allowed to officiate in a ceremonial way? Are the living fearful that it will soon be their turn to be on the cart? How has this affected their relationship to God—to each other? Nor must our attention fail to be brought to bear upon the bodies. Turn this picture upside down and look at the faces of the dead, particularly the body of the man on top. How long can those in burial details stay sane when encountering such scenes? To what can the human mind adjust? We can imagine such scenes being repeated in 148 camps throughout Europe, many on a far larger scale than we here see. The questions stagger. So does the silence which fails to fill the space left void where there are no answers. That is another tragedy of the Holocaust: there are no answers.

What is the point of having the signs here translated into English? The message is aimed for world wide consumption. We hate the Jews, and everyone else should too. Notice that the word "jewish" is not capitalized. Is there a message in that? (The word "German" used also as an adjective *is* capitalized). This isn't to be excused as some kind of picketing—this is intimidation. These youngsters, in terms of chronology but perhaps not of hatred, are stationary and they are wearing *that* uniform. It is expected that no good German, no loyal citizen, will buy here. Never mind that the store owner may have been a German war hero in Kaiser's army;

and never mind that he may have been employing many gentile clerks in his store, clerks whose jobs have immediately become jeopardized by demonstrations like this. What did these employees feel regarding the Nazi campaign? Were they so committed to the rightness of Hitler's cause that they gladly sacrificed their jobs for action against the enemy? Or did they think that things were going a little too far? If some were not in total agreement with the boycott policies, for reasons of personal economics or human rights or whatever, were they too frightened to publicly air their feelings? Did they simply "not want to get involved"? A close look at the two signs here indicates that they were printed. Nobody prints only two signs. We can be sure that many, many more of these were on show all over Germany. We can only wonder at how the Jews felt when they saw these words displayed. They all knew Jewish history, a history of persecutions suffered, but we know from how they *didn't* react that they had no concept of the magnitude of what awaited them. How could they have—the world would never let such a thing happen.

The sloppy oven area at Majdanek. There is a bent body-moving tool in the immediate foreground. How many Jews, Gypsies, Slavs, Russians, Poles, Latvians, Greeks and others did that device shove into the crematoria? How many different men operated that tool in their incendiary work? Sometimes the furnaces worked almost beyond capacity so that chimneys were in danger of collapsing. At Auschwitz, near the end of the war, 12,000 bodies a day were turned to ashes. That must have caused a frantic amount of energy to be spent on such activity. It took tremendous organization, fantastic coordination, awesome assembly line techniques to round up prisoners, ship them, kill them, remove the bodies from gas chambers, bring them to the ovens, keep the ovens burning at a constant pitch, put the bodies in, be certain that (for efficiency's sake) immediately upon destruction of corpses the doors could be opened again so that more cadavers could be put in. Time was of the essence. The war was coming to an end. German troop trains were being diverted from the front lines—where reinforcements were so badly needed—so

90

that more Jews could be transported to their deaths. Joseph
Goebbels died confident that, regardless of the outcome of the
war, the world would be grateful for the Nazi program of a
Final Solution to the universal problem of the Jews. Other
Nazi officials uttered similar thoughts. How can we respond
to this? Either the deaths of the 6,000,000 Jews and the
6,000,000 others in the camps are part of an event so
terrifying in history that we are utterly determined that such
acts must not happen again and that we each take individual
responsibility to fight, truly fight injustices everywhere or . . .
or . . .

An execution in Hungary. The man who is about to die is
striking a rather defiant pose. He is not trussed up to a pole,
not cringing from the irons that are about to penetrate his
body. Whatever he did to call a death sentence upon himself
does not appear to make him remorseful or so terrified that he
loses his dignity before the ultimate mystery. The police and
town officials gathered to witness this killing present a
curious picture. None of them are looking at the victim. This

is not true of the people in the left and right windows of the building which we face from our close up vantage point. The officer second from the left in the front row is looking away (as is another who is partially shielded from us by the rifles). Out of squeamishness? Shame? Does he recognize an injustice being done? Or is he looking around to make certain that everyone else is observing this example, this lesson being taught them so that these other men will not attempt to act contrary to fascist demands? The sandbags are not packed particularly high—the riflemen are obviously instructed not to aim for the man's head. That would be messy and additionally be somewhat dangerous with the possibility of ricocheting bullets. And we can see that the weapons indeed are aimed heart high. No doubt the town officials were being forced to witness this event. Only two seem to have bared their heads out of a kind of respect for death which that gesture implies. What was going on in the minds of the onlookers? Did they learn to love Big Brother equating that emotion with fear or were some vowing to fight the Nazis and their collaborators so that the man about to die will not have stood alone against corruption and human disintegration?

There are some who feel that the Holocaust must only be reacted to with silence. Words would somehow cheapen the event. Those of us who do not agree with this opinion are nevertheless often brought to silence when considering a scene such as this one. We can understand why the most effective Holocaust literature, meaning the autobiography, fiction and the poetry given their impulse from this event, is writing of understatement, of suggestion. One of the most significant of such works is *Night*, by Elie Wiesel. First published in Yiddish, the volume was over 800 pages long. In its revised form, it comes to less than 120 pages. The author, who in *Night* tells of his experiences at Auschwitz, where he lost his mother, sister and saw his father beaten to death, cut away and cut away at the original manuscript, but says that to the sensitive reader it is all still there. This is an important

concept for us if we are to grapple with the Holocaust on any meaningful level. As an author Wiesel is saying to us, "You try to complete what I present to you." There is a certain trust here (as there is in all great art, as there need be in all human relationships) and we must not betray that trust. The man holding the child's body in this photo may be attempting the same thing with us. We have only to look, no one need utter a word. Civilization has come to this—the horrors that can be perpetrated are reduced to a scene like this. Incomprehensible—certainly! But we are obligated to try to come as close as we can to understanding the un-understandable. Of the 11,000,000 victims of the Holocaust, perhaps 1,000,000 were children who had not yet reached their teens. As a human race we have been robbed of their love, their vivacity, their talents, their wisdom, their joy. We are considerably poorer for that. Maybe we didn't deserve them.

———————————

Again, the eyes have it, they hint at the depths of the event. They suggest the trauma of separation, of exile, of imprisonment for no crimes at all. Every visible face in this photograph is marked with tragedy. These people are on their way to a concentration camp where the series of shocks they will receive will kill some of them before they can be physically murdered. A view of the camp itself, with the guards, the dogs, the fences and barbed wire, the filthy barracks and above all the condition of the prisoners already there will provide a severe jolt to the psychological health of every man in this crowd. The exchange of clothing for prison attire—deliberately assigned so as not to fit (including the shoes used for long marches) in order to increase the sense of

humiliation—will provide another shock. The dehumanization process will continue as the men are stripped of their names and given numbers, indelibly tatooed on their arms, reminders that they are not persons, merely integers in the Nazi scheme of world domination. The shaving of the heads, of all bodily hair in fact, is another operation calculated to disorient a human being. So too are the beatings the prisoners will undergo as well as the remarks of abuse, threat, sexual innuendo and insult coming from those with the least bit of authority in the camps. (Many of these are criminals and sexual offenders, who were given charge over the Jews, Gypsies, Jehovah's Witnesses and others arbitrarily incarcerated.) Little pranks by the bathhouse staffers, such as the alternating of all cold or all hot water streams, will also cause confusion among the new prisoners. For the most part, the only thing they can be grateful for is that they have no mirrors in which to visibly see their own degradation. Many survivors were stunned to see themselves, almost unrecognizable, at the time they were freed by Allied troops.

When you think of train travel, what comes to mind? We complain when a train is late, get upset when the air conditioning (or heat) is off, we demand comfortable seating and expect rapid movement by the engineer. None of this applied to the Polish women here boarding a freight car in Cracow bound for death. They were packed standing on this winter ride with no possibility of heat. They may have been kept locked this way for several days, to be unloaded at the convenience of their captors. Sometimes, on such journeys, when the train would slow down near certain depots, free civilians would toss slices of bread into the narrow openings of the cars for the entertainment value of watching starving victims fight over the food. In one such case, a boy beat his own father to death to wrest the crumbs the old man had managed to obtain—and then the boy was killed by others who had witnessed the ghastly event. We can imagine the hysterical atmosphere of the trip. The riders had just been separated from their families, wrenched from their secure homes, dispossessed of nearly everything they owned, had been rounded up and kept waiting for who knows how long. They were frightened, abandoned and absolutely mystified. How many times must they have begun questions with the word "Why?" Answers could not be forthcoming. The Germans claimed to have certain answers, of course. But these satisfied no one, perhaps not even the Germans themselves. The Holocaust itself is a question of overwhelming magnitude, a nearly ultimate enigma with no possible answer. We can respond to it, but we cannot reason about it. That may be why modern philosophy has practically ignored its impact on contemporary thought and attitudes. And yet the question of the Holocaust will be ignored only at peril to the entire human race.

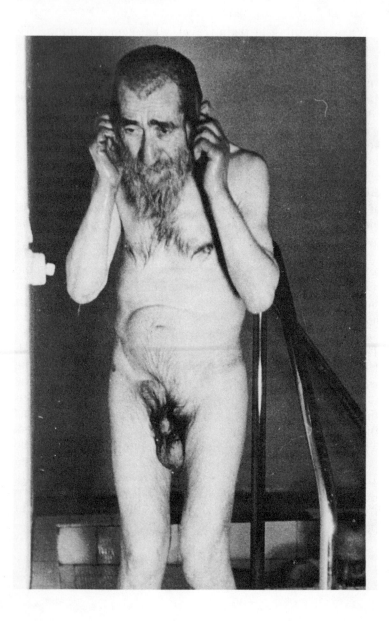

"Hey, Hans, let's have some sport. Bring your camera. We'll get this old Jew to make a fool of himself. It shouldn't be hard since all Jews are fools anyway. You, Jew, get over here. Strip. Immediately!" What were the threats which forced this man into this ignominious posture? How much had he seen that convinced him that to disobey might mean instant death or prolonged torture? There was no appeal from the whim of any camp authority, from the commandant down to criminals who were assigned as barracks chiefs. What is the enjoyment factor in ridiculing another human? Is physical superiority ever a basis for moral superiority? So many of the persecutors of the Jews called themselves Christians yet the Christ they claimed to follow never glorified force. Who is the finer human being, the city slicker who sells the country bumpkin the Brooklyn Bridge or the naive, trusting buyer who is willing to believe? Who is the finer human being, the guard who is tormenting the man here pictured or the man himself whose eyes, whose entire body, indicate some of the physical pain he is experiencing? The subject of mockery appears to be standing above floor level, perhaps atop some steps; this will serve as a makeshift stage for an audience of amused guards. Possibly other prisoners were forced to watch as well. Maybe this was part of a circus with a number of inmates forced into the big circle of attention. Did some resist, refuse? What happened to them? We can guess. Such entertainment had to come after 12-16 hour working shifts when the prisoners were exhausted and needed to rest. Slow or swift deaths were never enough for some of the Nazi authorities and their many collaborators. Kill them, yes, but take away their dignity first. To a devout Jew the privacy of the individual's body is beyond question. Michelangelo's angels were covered by protectors of the public's morality, but at Auschwitz, photographers acted differently with human beings.

Was the photographer pleased with this photograph? We can imagine the apprehension of the picture taker, after having run camera-rampant through Dachau. Maybe he went home and said to his wife, "I hope these pictures from Dachau come out. I got some real good ones today. They'll be very interesting if the developer doesn't mess them up." And when the final product was seen, did the photographer take pleasure in his achievement? Certainly this is not a great picture but there is a certain symmetry, a certain balance of line shown here with the upright cremators, the diagonal body, and building lines perpendicular to each other. We can see that this photograph is posed. The man on the right has his legs so positioned that he obviously is not walking. Possibly the cameraman asked them to stop in their tracks because his talented eye could recognize a dramatic shot when he saw one. What of the two men who are hauling the body? He on the right seems unwilling to cooperate with the photographer other than to halt when ordered—probably by a guard. The other man looks at the lens, but what is on his mind? Is he revenge minded, humiliated, angry, sad or just plain numb? It is not easy to tell from this shot. And the victim himself? The bones tell a portion of his suffering, but of course only a portion. He was nearly (if not totally) starved. But what of the humiliation he experienced while alive? What family tragedies did he witness before he himself became one? From this instant recorded in the picture, this man will be incinerated. He will have no burial place, there will be no grave over which some survivors may pray the *Kaddish*. In some of his fiction, Elie Wiesel symbolizes such persons as clouds in the sky. And stars as the eyes of dead children.

HARRY JAMES CARGAS

We've all heard humorous stories about children running from a gun toting farmer after stealing some of his produce and leaping over barbed wire leaving a little of themselves in the process. Bits of torn trousers on a barb can be a pretty funny sight to an onlooker. But children imprisoned by such wire can be a blasphemous vision as well. Here we see twelve youngsters separated from the world by wire meant for cattle and other beasts. They are a dozen out of approximately one million Jewish children exterminated by the Nazis and their very willing collaborators. Imagine, the future of European Jewry gassed, bayoneted, infants having their skulls crushed by being dashed against brick walls, shot, even burned alive in economy measures. Gas, after all, and bullets, too, cost money. So these children behind barbed wire were being prepared for death. They seem to have just been incarcerated. They do not appear to have been starved for as long as the children we see in other photos. Of course, young boys and girls were not kept alive very long in the camps; they were non-productive, ever an emotional drain on their elders. Hence they were usually executed quickly. They can be taken for a normal group. On the extreme right there is the neighborhood fat boy, the one everybody pokes fun at. In front of him the child looks street-wise; perhaps he's the group leader. While everyone else is facing the camera, he's more independently looking in another direction. Some of the children are tall, others not; some are obviously more frightened than others. The one in the middle, fifth from the left, seems ready to cry. Can we show such a photograph to our own children? Could we make them understand why these little Isaacs will be sacrificed and why this time God's angel will not intervene to rescue them?

Franz Fanon did some important work on the effect that torture had on those who performed it in Algeria. His conclusions are quite clear. Those French officials who brutally mistreated Arabs in the systematic way that they did, themselves suffered psychological harm. There seems to be little evidence, however, that Nazi persecutors were troubled in the same way. Dr. Carl Clauberg, shown here, is an example. The chief physician of a women's clinic in a hospital in Upper Silesia, this man worked on a scheme for sterilizing Jewish women, a procedure which became known as the "Clauberg method." His plan was to inject the victims with an irritating solution but without indicating to them the nature of this experiment. He hoped to be able to sterilize 1,000 Jewish women per day. Working at Auschwitz, and far from being remorseful, there is evidence that Dr. Clauberg liked to show off his experiments. After the war, and following a prison term in Russia, Clauberg was eager to tell reporters that he had perfected his sterilization method and that he looked forward to its being used in "special cases." After a full decade of opportunities for reflection leading to remorse, Clauberg was still very proud of his achievement. He is not unique. We hear of Nazi war veterans having annual reunions and some of them celebrating their sub-human exploits. Ironically, while we regularly hear of Holocaust survivors committing suicide, we never hear of their tormentors doing the same. Psychiatrists have discussed the guilt feelings of the survivors—a kind of "Why was I saved and the others not?" question bothers all of them. We have no record of comparable feelings on the part of the truly guilty, the criminals who implemented the Hitlerian program. The photo here of Clauberg seems to show a comfortable individual, content with what he has to do in life, even proud of it. What ever happened to conscience?

105

Bodies piled upon bodies piled upon bodies. How ever was anyone able to adjust to such sights? How could those soldiers who manned the machine guns light up cigarettes during their fifteen minute breaks from murder? How did the men who operated the bulldozers, which swept mounds of corpses into pits for mass burial, escape nightmares each time they went to sleep—and escape "daymares" too? Why is it that we repeatedly hear of the suicides of survivors but we almost never hear of the persecutors committing acts of self destruction (unless when captured and brought to trial)? But there is another direction towards which questions may be aimed—not questions meant to blame or condemn, but ones which trouble survivors themselves as well as the rest of us. For example: How is it possible for prisoners at Auschwitz or Dachau or Buchenwald to keep on functioning in the face of all of the brutality they see and they suffer? How, when on a march to work, and when your neighbor beside you drops from exhaustion and is immediately shot by an impatient guard, do you keep on marching as if it were quite an ordinary thing to do? We can imagine the conversations taking place in the barracks at night—no, we don't have to imagine them, because survivors have told us of the talk that went on at the end of a work day. "Who died today?" "How many did we lose on the road?" "When they beat Max, did he die or is he still alive?" Almost matter of fact inquiries that today horrify the survivors themselves who consider to what they had been reduced. And yet they went on, and they did survive, and we can bless them for that. As Terrence Des Pres has noted, for too long we have only glorified the dead as heroes and we must recognize those who endured through the Holocaust as true heroes as well.

We hesitate to identify the pair in this photograph as children. Chronologically they are—perhaps five and ten years old. But experientially they are old, far older than perhaps anyone ever ought to be. They are living through their own suffering and they are the inheritors of the suffering of their people. This is a centuries old persecution and it has registered in the sadness of their eyes. We like to see our young people smiling and full of hope. But there is none of that found here but rather defeat, resignation. There is not even a trace of the question "Why?" in this scene. This boy and this girl are beyond framing questions in their minds. Instead they appear to be observers. Theirs is a "What next?" attitude. They have already been taken away from their homes, their comfortable and comforting bedrooms, their neighborhoods, friends, schools, parents, grandparents. Possibly they saw some of their loved ones beaten, murdered. Certainly they saw their authority figures (fathers and mothers, rabbis, teachers) disenfranchised in one swift stroke. All sense of security must have vanished for them in an instant. How did they take it? How did they adjust? In part, they must have been numbed. Look at their faces. Notice their hands, also, the fingers hooked onto the fence not with any sense of purpose, but as expressive of despair as the eyes. What are these two old children seeing? What has brought a crowd to the fence? Our imaginations may run riot and yet they might not approach the true reality. We know this from eyewitness accounts of what took place during the roundup of the Jews. The crimes of these two children? They are enemies of the Third Reich. They are marked for destruction.

A picture of Adolf Hitler is in itself an atrocity photograph for many. Some have said that the motivation for his acts was that he was humiliated in having found out that he was part Jewish (not true); that his quest for power stemmed from sexual abberation (possible); that he was mad (doubtless). His attitude toward Jews, which reflected the attitude of many Germans and others throughout centuries, are mirrored in these few—of many which could be selected—quotations from his best selling book, *Mein Kampf* (My Fight). The references in these quotations are always to Jews. "Their whole existence is an embodied protest against the aesthetics of the Lord's image." "Was there any form of filth or profligacy, particularly in cultural life, without at least one Jew involved in it?" "Existence compels the Jew to lie, and to lie perpetually, just as it compels the inhabitants of the northern countries to wear warm clothing." The Jew "is and remains the typical parasite, a sponger who like noxious bacillus keeps spreading as soon as a favorable medium invites him." "Hence today I believe that I am acting in accordance with the will of the Almighty Creator: *by defending myself against the Jew, I am fighting for the work of the Lord*" (Hitler's italics). ". . . The inferior being—and this is the Jew." ". . . . To my deep and joyful satisfaction, I had at last come to the conclusion that the Jew was no German." "Only the Jew can praise an institution which is as dirty and false as he himself." ". . . The Jew robbed the whole nation and pressed it beneath his domination . . ." "And so the Jew today is the great agitator for the complete destruction of Germany." Hitler's words are not pleasant reading, but they are necessary reading. His emotionally pitched remarks are versions of the kinds of things people have been saying about their "enemies" from the beginning of history. When will we learn to see each other as human beings, as brothers and sisters, perhaps in disagreement, but as brothers and sisters?

Dare we attempt to provide a biography for this incinerated corpse? Christians did that sort of thing concerning the
early martyrs of their faith. The bones of a young child were
found in the Roman catacombs and as a tradition grew about
them, she was given the name Philomena and eventually was
revered by some as St. Philomena. Biographies were written
about her. Recently these life stories were found to be without
substance and the Vatican so pronounced. Yet such "poetic"
biographies are not hard to construct. We know something
about the lives of young Roman girls, about early Christians,
about existence in the catacombs. A pretty authentic "novel"
could then be built around such a character. We might do the
same for this victim. We know enough to make a convincing
plot on just a few facts. If we can ascertain this person's sex,
nationality and approximate age, we might be able to
synthesize a life story. No doubt, like most Holocaust victims,
this person would have led a rather ordinary life until the
Nazi program gained momentum. But then the term "ordinary" was stripped of any possible application to the

experience that this woman or man was subject to. And for us, looking on in anguished wonder, this person takes on a kind of meaning with which no one ought to be burdened. This is indeed a troubling photograph. We may feel troubled not only when contemplating the corpse, but also in thinking about the living Red Cross man. This scene appears to have been posed for the cameraman. We are justified in wondering why. Does the onlooker have a function? Is he there to register an emotion for us which a propagandist wants to be certain that we somehow achieve? Does someone worry that we will not know how to react? Is somebody afraid that we will become numbed too easily?

We have no information about this photograph. Yet we can be certain that it was not taken at the end of World War II, at liberation time. The reason for our certainty is simple: no such large number of old women could have survived any Nazi camp. Since they were not productive workers, and were thus an economic drag—they had to be fed (however meager the rations were), housed, guarded.... Yes, guarded.

These grandmothers were forcibly retired into the ultimate old age homes of Dachau, Auschwitz, Treblinka. For those of us who are becoming increasingly restless in the company of our aging parents, Hitler and Eichmann and Himmler and Hoess have suggested a solution. Kill them. If this sounds obscene, we need only remember that the world stood by, virtually in disbelief, later in absolutely guilty inaction, while these grandmothers were being gassed, starved, shot, burned or buried alive. We can also guess from the clothing the women are wearing that they have just recently been taken prisoner. Their garb is not in tatters, they appear to have enough to keep relatively warm (although the woman on the left, closest to the camera, might not agree). But the stunning aspect of this scene is in the age of most of the prisoners. No doubt most of these women have earned a right to a comparatively easy old age. Imagine your grandmother in such a camp, forced to endure long roll calls while standing out in the cold, subject to bodily searches. Could she negotiate the trip each night to the top row of bunks. Could she manage to crawl down safely in the dark to go to the bathroom? Would she have any desire to go on living when separated from the rest of her family, not knowing if her kin are alive or dead? The expression on the face of the woman on the right, near the camera, may answer all of these questions.

———

Hip deep in bodies, that's what these reluctant prisoners are. Well, *somebody* has to stack them. Indeed they are stacked, not indiscriminately strewn around the railroad car. This orderly arrangement allows for maximum utilization of space. Therefore, time is saved, energy is conserved. This is good for the Nazi war effort. Fewer trips by train will have to be made. How did these two men first take to their job? We can picture various work assignments given to prisoners, and this pair got this task. Actually, it tells us a little about them. For one thing, we know that they are reasonably healthy, reasonably strong, else they would not have been selected for

this work. From this we may further conclude that they are probably fairly new prisoners, since almost none who were in the camps for any length of time remained somewhat healthy and somewhat strong. So how did they react to this job? How did they talk about it between themselves? With others? In order to cope, psychologically, did they have to resort to a grim humor to keep from collapsing in despair? Did they have to block out seeing these corpses as the bodies of human beings and simply treat each one as an inanimate unit of cargo like a brick or board or slab of meat? Did they have the experience of being brought up short in their work, as others in their position were, because they recognized one of the corpses as that of a dead brother or grandfather? (This happened so many times.) Or did they come across mangled, emaciated corpses, unidentifiable, which reminded them of loved ones, which put doubts into their minds as to whether or not these were members of their families? Perhaps one of these men may have felt that he thus encountered his own father ten thousand times.

"Efficiency" is a key word in the Nazi vocabulary. Nothing must be wasted. Hence all Jewish property was expropriated by the Nazis in the territories which they occupied. When they got their prisoners to camp, they were shorn of all bodily hair. Literally mountains of human hair were collected and transformed into rugs and other items of warmth for the conquerors. The grizzly topic of soap made from human flesh can never be forgotten in this context. (We do not mention decorations made from human skin, such as lampshades, because such actions were taken more for entertainment rather than efficiency's sake.) Then too there were the medical experiments, a hideous lot of them, which were performed on the bodies of persons who "were going to die anyway." There's a ghastly element of efficiency in *that*, as well. So we are not surprised, then, at collections of eyeglasses or of artificial limbs taken from the myriads of people who will no longer be able to use them. It was the job of some prisoners, remember, to extract gold from the teeth of the dead. The Nazis were experts at recycling nearly everything.

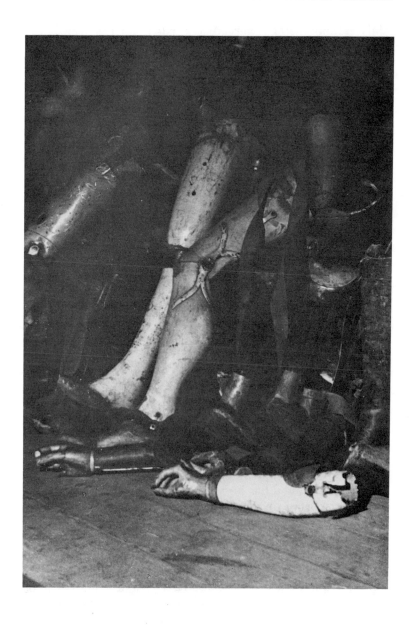

Only human beings were disregarded. As the war effort became more demanding it was determined that bullets were too expensive to be wasted on killing the 6,000,000 Jews and the 6,000,000 others—even at the rate of one bullet per victim. Zyklon B, a cheap gas, was put forth by some proud chemist as an efficient answer to the wasteful problem. Others helped the war effort in an even more severely economic mode, by burning prisoners alive, or burying them without their having first died. People tumbled all over themselves with such suggestions which were highly appreciated. Such people can't even hide behind the excuse that "I was just following orders."

This photograph was taken at the time of liberation. The man on the ground has just learned that he will not be on the first transport of prisoners going to an Allied army hospital. He seems devastated by the news. This scene is a reminder of the suffering that all survivors of the Holocaust will experience all of the rest of their lives, even though they will dwell in comparative freedom. Some survivors will never be able to bring themselves to ride on a train again. Many will be pained at merely hearing the German language spoken. Often, we are told by the survivors themselves and by psychia-

trists working with some of them, people experience feelings of guilt for having lived while so many others were unable to. There is a complex variety of reasons for these guilt feelings but often survivors will tell you that so many good people perished and "through some stroke of luck I did not." We must not wonder at the vehemence of their reaction when they hear that the American Nazi Party is planning a march in their community or their refusal to laugh at Holocaust jokes. Suicides among survivors are abnormally high—but the word "abnormal" applies to so much of their existence. Even their children, as an ever growing body of testimony indicates to us, have become victims in a way and their lives have been scarred by the experiences of their parents, whom they know, and their grandparents, aunts, uncles and other family members whom they can only envision as ashes. Family reunions are not very large among the families of survivors. No one has yet done a study on the suicides of survivors but we cannot help wondering if we have failed them in serious ways.

What does the G.I. think as he looks down in the grave at dead babies after liberation at Nordhausen? There was no liberation for these children, unless death itself may be seen so. But it is blasphemous for those of us who live to see the deaths of others in such a "positive" way. A Christian minister was heard to say, thirty years after Auschwitz, that theologically speaking, the 6,000,000 Jews are better off dead than alive. That's some theology! Why not kill people right after they are baptized, when their souls are in the purest state they can ever be, according to theology? Another Christian minister, at a convention of editors in the religious press field, argued for over three hours (while imbibing scotches in a plush hotel hospitality room) why we had to slaughter the Indians to bring them to Christ. Better known is the remark of the U.S. General who explained the annihilation of a Vietnamese village as an act engaged in to save the inhabitants from Communism. The Nazis, we know, wanted to save the world from something too—from Jews and their iniquitous conspiracy to control the whole world. Something about Jewish *blood* was so threatening that no attempt would ever be made to save boys and girls for a massive re-education program into "Aryan thought." Instead, even they were subject to death by murder. Eyewitnesses tell us not only of babies being starved, and shot (used as targets on some occasions), and gassed, and burned, and buried alive, but of babies being thrown in the air to come down on the points of bayonets, of having their heads bashed against the walls or the ground, of being tossed to killer dogs. These are truly equilibrium destroying facts. All of us are different because "ordinary" people like ourselves were able to perform such atrocities—or be silent while they happened.

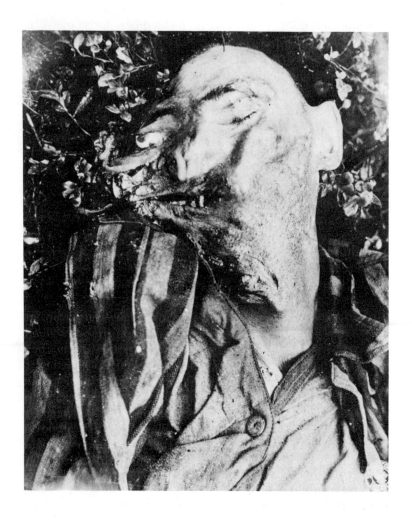

This was a face. It is grotesque, reminding us of novelist Flannery O'Connor's reply to a question about the bizarre situations and characters she rendered to present her theological viewpoint. She insisted that to the hard of hearing you have to shout. The photograph here is a response to those who would hail war as a noble effort, or worse, who would deny that the Holocaust ever really happened. Since over forty books in Europe and the United States have been published denying the actuality of Nazi tortures, let the author study this picture. This man was beaten to death with a hammer. Who was he? When he was nursing in his mother's arms, what hopes did she have for him when he reached maturity? Did she dream that he would become a medical doctor who might perform heroic acts of healing? Perhaps she hoped that her baby would become a rabbi and attend the spirit rather than the body. Possibly the boy would be trained as a scientist, become a good family man. He may have been a father. It is not impossible that a son of his saw him being bludgeoned to death. Surely the mother could not have dared to imagine her son's cruel end; he has become, for the world, only a victim, his face and head bones crushed because some guard was somehow irritated with him. And what of the guard? Was he mad or sane in the way the world ordinarily judges? When he finished his human massacre, was he able to look upon his effort or did it disgust him? Did he brag about his heroics or was he as ashamed of himself as we are of him now? This was a face, the face of a man who lived, and dreamed and died a ghastly death. We cannot look at this face—and yet we dare not avert our eyes lest . . .

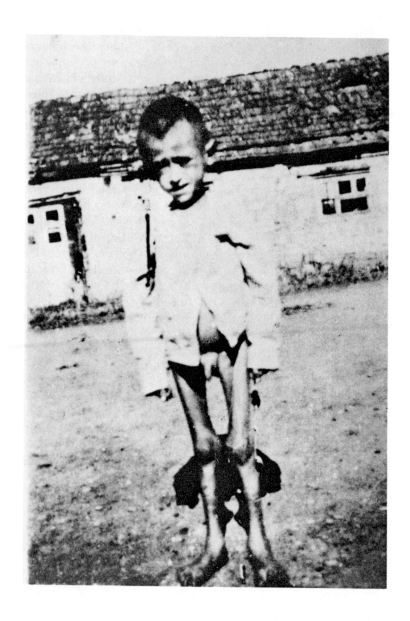

Could this be one of those children? We might ask this question when we hear the following story. There were certain occasions when Nazi troops would intrude on an "enemy" family and hold them all at gunpoint. Then, pretending to be moved by the tears and pleading of the wife-mother of the home, the soldier in charge of the unit would offer to show mercy. Since the woman had three sons and a husband, only two of them would be taken away to their deaths. *She* must choose which two. Is this one of those children? The woman had to choose, else all four males would die. The agony of the moment (regardless of the numbers of males involved) is probably beyond imagination. On what basis would she make her selection? What possible bases can there be for such a choice? Who, having made such a choice, would not go mad in contemplating it afterwards? We even know of one such instance in which the Nazis gave a mother a choice between four sons, then went counter to that choice and took the two sons away whom she had selected to live. Could this be one of those children? What was the relationship between the mother and her two remaining boys in this instance? What kind of a ghoul does it take to wrench such torturous decisions while acting under the guise of a human being? And yet, if we say that such soldiers were less than human, we would be saying that they are exonerated from judgment because they are not fully responsible for their acts. Somehow, at least emotionally, this seems completely unacceptable. We become aware how vast a spectrum of behavior the concept of humanity covers. We become aware, too, of how vast a failure civilization has been in certain areas. This little boy, before the barracks of Auschwitz, shows it all.

The only way out of the suffering for most Jews during the Holocaust was through death. Millions upon millions perished at the hands of those who unilaterally chose the side of the foe. Some victims, however, in their despair, terminated their own lives. Theorizing about the morality of suicides becomes nearly blasphemous in the face of the desperation of the inmates at Auschwitz, Buchenwald, Dachau, Treblinka and the other institutions of physical and personality annihilations. Moral standards are, after all, meant to apply to normal life situations. While we may cavil about certain dilemmas which women and men are plunged into during the course of earthly existence, it seems impossible to categorize the Holocaust events as anything but abnormal—subnormal. It may not be too strong a judgment to say that the Ten Commandments did not apply to the victims at Auschwitz. Jews and other prisoners were constantly brutalized, were literally treated as things by sadistic guards in a system created specifically for such behavior possibilities. People were hungry, ill, dislocated, despairing over the loss of loved ones and home, frightened, exhausted, covered with their own feces and often with filth of those who slept above them on bunk beds. We can have a slight idea of the conditions when we remember that psychiatrist Viktor Frankl refused to wake up fellow inmates who were having nightmares because he felt that the reality to which he would be bringing the dreamer back was worse than the sleeping mind could conjure. The man in this photograph had to deliberately transverse through a warning zone to voluntarily throw his body onto electrically charged barbed wire. A number of inmates sought release this way. Equally depressing is the knowledge that a significant number of survivors of the Holocaust have committed suicide.

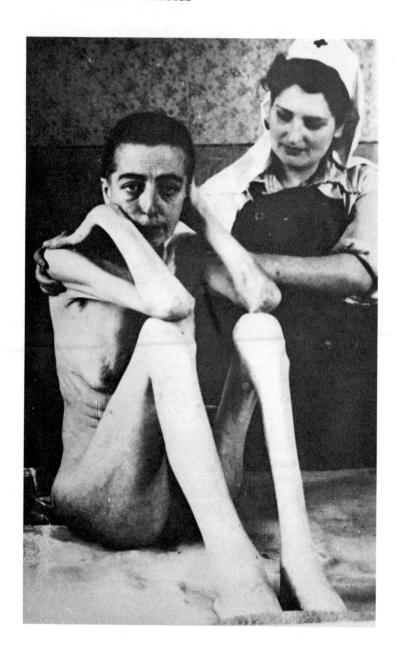

This woman has survived Auschwitz. Can we have even a slight understanding of what that might mean? Her hair had begun to grow back, but not her flesh. We can only hope that the Red Cross woman assisting her knows how to be of help. We read that probably thousands of survivors died because liberating troops, in undisciplined compassion, overfed the starving camp inmates and thereby poisoned them. There are no more tragic examples of irony than that. Some Jewish survivors went back to their home towns expecting to be greeted with welcome. Instead, they were shot to death by people who called themselves Christians. This appears to have happened more in Poland than anywhere else. Many Polish Jews were rounded up because they were betrayed to the Nazis. Their price was not even thirty pieces of silver, often merely a bottle of whiskey. Jews who escaped the concentration camp were sometimes gunned down by Polish partisans who were also fighting the common enemy, the Germans. And then there are the Jews who struggled through the entire Holocaust experience, only to be murdered after the war when they tried to go back home. One Jewish woman who now lives in the United States, when asked if she ever wished to return to her native land for a visit, answered abruptly, "Never. Poland to me is blood." Of approximately 3,000,000 Jews in Poland before the Second World War, 2,700,000 lost their lives. Today it is estimated that only about 6,000 Jews can be found in Poland. Is this woman among the 6,000? Given the story that her eyes hint at, we can doubt it. But the geographic location that this woman may have chosen to settle in is not of great import. What she underwent is. So is the fact that people of all backgrounds, classes and types, aided in forcing that experience on her.

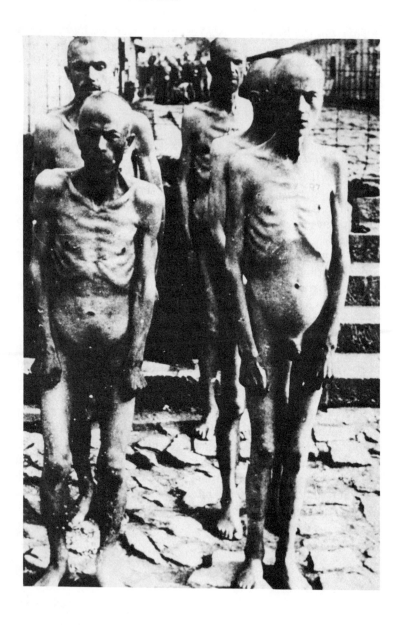

The scowl and clenched fists of the man front left of this snapshot are a tribute to the human spirit. We may not be as free as we would like to be in our actions, but we *are* free in our ability to respond to what is happening to us. This man's response to his humiliation is clear and unmistakable. Like millions of others, these men pictured here were forced to endure roll call. They were often made to stand naked for hours in the most inclement weather. If they fell from exhaustion—and why wouldn't many of them, looking at their shrinking bodies—they were shot. Their guards might beat and otherwise torture them just for amusement. The collar bone of the short man protrudes in a sickening manner; his shoulder angle makes it appear that he may have been seriously injured and must stand awkwardly. There are true stories of prisoners who survived the Nazi camps who were several inches shorter than when they entered the barracks. One such man had his back broken by a Nazi soldier's rifle butt, and the prisoner kept on working immediately because he knew that if he showed incapacitation he was doomed. Look at the ground on which these men were forced to stand. Not very comfortable. Nothing in their lives in the camps ever was. Maybe this is just a snapshot by a Nazi soldier who wanted to have a momento of his authority? We can be sure that the men were ordered not to try to hide their nakedness with their hands. And naked indeed they are. All bodily hair has been removed. This had the double effect of obtaining "raw material" to aid the German war effort and to further humiliate prisoners. Note that the two men whose chests are visible on the right have had their identification numbers tatooed onto their chests.

The bodies of Jewish victims of the Holocaust at Wobbelin, a branch camp of Nevengamme in Germany: who is responsible? No one can answer that because anti-Semitism has been a single line historical process which began with expropriation of Jewish property, led to forced exile of Jews, to programs, ghettoization and finally a concerted effort at genocide. The following remarks will put the Holocaust in its horrid context:

God hates the Jews and always hated the Jews. —St. John Crysostom.

The peoplehood of the Jews has been cancelled. —St. Cyprian.

Jews were delivered up by God as deserters from His law. —Marcus Minucius Felix.

When was the Jew not the transgressor of the law? —Tertullian.

Observe the day of the Sabbath, not after a sensual fashion, not as the Jews, whose delight is to spend their leisure in evil pursuits. —St. Augustine.

Their synagogue or school is to be set on fire . . . Their

houses are to be torn down and destroyed in the same way . . . They are to have all their prayer bodies and Talmudics taken from them . . . Whoever hears the name of God from a Jew shall report him to the authorities or throw pig droppings on him. —Martin Luther.

Emancipation from the yoke of Judaism appears to us the foremost necessity. —Richard Wagner.

Emancipation from usury and money, that is from practical, real Judaism, would constitute the emancipation of our time. —Karl Marx.

After the death of Christ Israel was dismissed from the service of Revelation. —Cardinal Michael von Faulhaber.

The inferior being—this is the Jew. —Adolf Hitler.

There is no innocent blood of Jewish children in the world. All Jewish blood is guilty. You have to die. —A Papal Nuncio, 1944.

[Silence] —Pope Pius XII.

From our perspective there is a comic element in this greeting between two conspirators at the camp bearing the dreaded name of Dachau. But there is absolutely nothing humorous about the war business in which these men engaged. Hitler had a dream; he convinced a significant number of persons of the validity of that vision; and fifty million people lost their lives as a direct result. Fifty million people. Here are two of the leaders of the implementation of Hitler's plan. Perhaps Heinrich Himmler, on the right, is congratulating a colleague for a job well done—a job of extermination. We know that Himmler often did just that to underlings who carried out the Nazi murderous policies particularly well. Himmler might have remained a rather successful poultry farmer had it not been for his friendship with Hitler. Instead, he became the head of the Fuehrer's personal body guard, the S.S. In four years, mainly through his organizational talents, Himmler brought membership in his elite corps to 50,000, up from a mere 300. Throughout much of World War II, Himmler was clearly the number two

134

power in all of the Third Reich. Among his major tasks—and look at the face of this true terrorist, described by some as having "the look of an intelligent schoolteacher"—was the elimination of "racial degenerates": those Jews, Poles, Czechs, Russians and all others who stood in the way of German progress. When Himmler lost his leader's confidence, he tried to make peace with the Allies, but the war's end found him trying to escape detection through a disguise. He was apprehended, however, and died a suicide. A far cry from the momentarily triumphant man shown here, a man with, as one who knew him said, "slender, pale and almost girlishly soft hands covered with blue veins."

Many Jews asked where God was at the time of the World War II persecutions. This man, perhaps a rabbi, is forced to carry his symbol of God like an albatross around his neck. Both he and his religion are being ridiculed. In some concentration camps, Jews, who have a long and honorable tradition of dialoguing and even of disputing with God, put the Creator of the universe on trial. The verdicts varied. In some instances, God was found guilty of having broken his covenant, his agreement, his promise to his chosen people. In at least one case an opposite conclusion was reached. Those sitting in on the judgment, having heard and deliberated on and prayed over the evidence, concluded that what Jews were undergoing collectively were the birth pangs of the coming of the Messiah, the long awaited Savior of a world long in need of salvation. Those of us who are not Jewish have another question: Where was Christ at Auschwitz? The death camps rose in the midst of a Christian civilization. How could this have happened? Where was Christian witness, except on a small, ineffectual scale? Where were the official churches? Why were so many silent? Why were so many cooperative? And after the question of Christ at Auschwitz, another has been posed. Where was man? Indeed, where was humanity when inhumanity ruled in Europe? In fact, where is humanity now, after the Holocaust? Have we learned enough from the horrors of that time? Or are Biafra, Indonesia, the Central African Empire, Paraguay, Vietnam, Brazil, Uganda, Iran, Hungary, Lebanon, Ireland all evidence that the spirit which endowed the Holocaust lives yet? Are we willing to passively accept this as our nature, or will we work to resist evil in all its forms? If we do not, then all of us will be able to do no more than wear our gods like albatrosses on our own breasts.

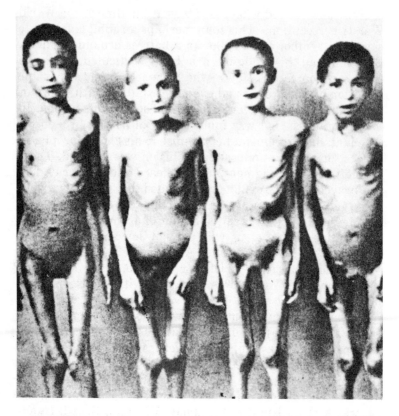

These boys ought to be posing for a picture from summer camp. They are of an age where they should be carefree, laughing, unconcerned with the travail of the world. Instead they are forced to stand for a photograph from another kind of camp, one which is the gruesome antithesis of the kinds of locations we strive to send our children to. There are no smiles on these faces; there is no hint of merriment in the eyes—old before their time. At a period when young bodies must have proper nourishment for growth and future benefits, these youngsters are being fed on a cup of weak soup daily. Any child who stole a second cup was subject to death. Elie Wiesel has written of a boy who was caught doing just that. All of the prisoners were called out to witness the hanging. The victim's body was so emaciated, so light, that it could not aid him to die quickly at the end of the rope. He struggled with life for over a half hour before he expired. In his memoir, *Night*, Wiesel wrote that after that, the soup tasted of corpses to him. The agonizing death happened to a child much like the four pictured here. No doubt these youngsters were incarcerated in reasonably good health. Perhaps one or two of them was even overweight. But now we only have to look at their legs, their knees, their ribs, to know of the kind of diet they had suffered over a period of time. Besides malnutrition, such boys and girls experienced many other diseases. The only way for some of them to earn livable rations was to become the sexual favorite of a camp pervert who had some authority. This didn't guarantee longevity, merely a little fuller stomach. Children of this age need the love, protection, wisdom, security of their parents and it was denied to them. How did they feel about their parents during the crisis? Did the boys and girls feel betrayed, abandoned? Or did they somehow have some understanding of the incomprehensible?

Of over 140 prison and death camps erected under Nazi rule, only 18 were in Germany. Poland hosted 48. Lest we forget where these camps flourished, *flourished!* here is a listing.

Austria	Ebensee, Gusen, Mauthausen
Belgium	Breendonck, Malines
Bulgaria	Somovit
Czechoslovakia	Novaky, Patronka, Petrzalka, Terezin, Zilina
Estonia	Aigali, Ereda, Goldfield, Kalevi, Klooga, Lagedi, Liiva, Vaivara
France	Agde, Argeles-sur-mer, Barcares, Beaune la Rodande, Camp du Richard, Compiegne, Drancy, Fort-Barraux, Gurs, Les Milles, Natzweiler-Struthof, Nexon, Pithiviers, Saint-Cyprien
Galacia	Borislav, Buchach, Lvov, Plaszow
Germany	Arbeitsdorf, Bergen-Belsen, Bochum,

Brunswick, Buchenwald, Cottbus, Dachau, Dora, Esterwegen, Flossenburg, Grossrosen, Lichtenburg, Nevengamme, Niederhagen, Oranienburg, Ravensbruck, Sachsenhausen, Wells

Greece Haidon

Hungary Kistarcsa

Italy Bolzano, Fossoli, Mantua, Raab

Latvia Kaiserwald, Salaspils

Libya Giado, Homs

Lichtenburg Lichtenburg

Lithuania Kaunas, Ponary

Netherlands Amersfoort, Vught, Westerbork

Poland Auschwitz, Belzec, Belzyce, Birkenau, Bogusze, Bronna Gora, Budzyn, Burggrabben, Chelmno, Chodosy, Chryzanow, Ciezanow, Elbing, Gerdaven, Heiligenbeil, Jaktorow, Jesau, Karczew, Kelbasin, Kielce, Kosaki, Lackie Wielkie, Majdanek, Miedzyrzec Podalski, Mielec, Mlyniewo, Nisko, Peikinia, Plew, Pomiechowek, Praust, Radomsko, Sasov, Schippenbeil, Seerapen, Skarzysko-Kamienna, Sobibor, Stolp, Stutthof, Thorn, Treblinka, Tyszowce, Zaglebia, Zaprudy, Zaslaw, Zawarnice, Zbaszyn

Rumania Caracal, Markulesci

Russia Akmechetka, Bogdanovka, Bratslav, Domanevka, Golta, Kamenka-Bugskaya, Koldychevo, Maly Trostinek, Odessa, Paczara, Sekiryani, Targu-Jiu, Tiraspol, Vapnyarka, Volkoysk, Yedintsy, Zborov

Yugoslavia Ada, Djakovo, Jadovna, Jasenovac, Loborgrad, Saymishte

Here we see Hitler youth supervising the humiliation of Viennese Jews. Nazi psychology was profound in many ways. Indoctrinate the young very early. Teach them whom to hate and what to do about it. They heard the Nazi chant, "Germany wake up, Judah drop dead" and the famous battle cry, "Hep! Hep! Hep! Death and destruction to all the Jews." Hitler himself told the world in his bestselling book, *Mein Kampf* (which was so successful that it made him an independently wealthy man—let us reflect on that!), that people could be made to believe anything if they were told to in the "right" way. It was he who observed in this volume, written during the eight months that he spent in prison for his part in the famed Munich Beer-Hall *putsch*, that the bigger the lie, the easier it will be for the public to swallow. And if one lie, why not others? Thus the Nazis were able to effectively use the Jews as scapegoats. It was they who caused the downfall of Germany in World War I; it was they who, as a part of a world wide conspiracy, helped to keep Germany economically depressed; it was they who tainted the sacred Aryan blood with their own impurities, hence Jewry had to be extinguished. Fanatics came to believe that Adolf Hitler was the third person of the Christian Trinity—Hitler was called by some the Holy Ghost. The next step is a rather simple one: if one of the members of the triune Godhead indicates that Jews are God's enemies, then the true faithful are merely doing holy work when they kill the Jews. And of course starting the "believers" young will help assure success. Notice the number of children in this photograph who are involved in the goings on by way of holding hands to keep the crowd from overflowing into the arena of humiliation. How clever for someone to have arranged for the youngsters to get a close up view.

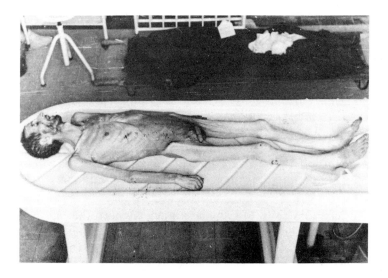

Medical experiments, conducted by doctors who had taken oaths not to misuse the knowledge which they had acquired at universities, were performed with tragic frequency. These traitors to humanity conducted experiments to see if typhus could be controlled, to find out if the human system could somehow absorb sea-water, to determine how bodies react to

143

high altitude and others to extremely low temperature. The effects of jaundice, injected from infected animals into human systems, were tested. Other experiments included mass sterilization, studying the effects of mustard gas, and the collection of Jewish skulls for traces of racial inferiority. One of the more hideous of a host of hideous laboratory investigations had to do with the transplant of human bones which were taken from Polish women in Ravensbruck. The doctor who lectured, with pride, to an audience of doctors on his work, was not challenged by any in that gathering. Operations were inflicted on Gypsies to try to prove their blood is different from German blood. We cannot fail to insist that these monstrous acts were conceived by doctors, approved by other doctors and carried out by still other doctors, many of whom were decorated for their services to what was to become the Thousand Year Reich. The isolated suffering which many of the victims underwent is symbolized by this photograph. What must it be like to die alone while being tortured? Can anyone maintain hope for self or the universe under such conditions? Or does one even have such thoughts at a time like that? Perhaps the physical pain is so overwhelming that a man or woman can only give attention to that pain. And the many, many experimenters—how did they feel? Were some euphoric in such assignments, happy to be serving Adolf Hitler, confident in the knowledge that their supply of human guinea pigs was practically endless?

We hear dialogue in gangster movies where the bad guy threatens to blow somebody's head off. The audience never treats this kind of talk seriously and on occasion it can bring snickers from the viewers. The reality, as we see in this scene, is nothing to be laughed at, however. It is sickening, sickening. All of us, at times, contemplate our own deaths. Teenagers will ask each other, "How would you rather die, by drowning, being shot or hanged?" Few of us could envision ending up like the man in the center of this photograph, with his forehead ripped off by a machine gun bullet. Death was mercifully instantaneous to him while being horrendous and

ugly to us, the viewers. These murdered men are being humiliated, the killers believe, even in death. Their sex organs are exposed as if, somehow, the victims can be demeaned even more. What has happened, instead, is that all humanity is demeaned by both the killings and the exposures of the bodies. We are all less because these things have happened. If we think about the lives of three men here, we wonder about their hopes for the future; what did they enjoy in life; how much trouble did they cause? Were they normal, every day kind of guys? Perhaps they were, in life but not in death. Even though deaths somewhat like each of theirs were to be shared by 11,000,000 other children, women and men, each death was unique too. In fact, all deaths are unique. But the photograph here evokes a kind of terror in us because not only of the intrinsic horror of the scene but also because of our inability to gain any understanding of what happened. Within the contexts of the various philosophies and theologies extant, the Holocaust is meaningless. We have no framework for comprehending the awe-ful event. How is it permitted that this helpless man's head was blown off? How is it that some *one* could actually commit such an act?

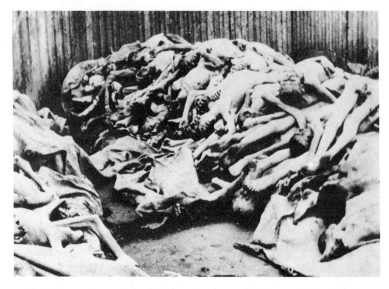

As we contemplate this scene, we might consider the story of Doctor Yaffa Eliach, who tells about her experience as a child survivor of a death camp. Liberation came for her when she was eleven or twelve years old. She emigrated from Europe to Palestine. Not long after arriving in that British governed territory, she accompanied her parents to a funeral. She remembers having asked two questions of her father. "Where are the other bodies?" and "Who killed this person?" At the threshold of teenagedom, little Yaffa Eliach did not know that people died one at a time and she did not know that people could die natural deaths. Her own life experience did not lead her to know anything else. With scenes like the one shown here vivid in her mind, we can understand how this would be so in her life. The shape of the ongoing psychological tragedy of the Holocaust, for the survivors, is so grotesquely different from anything that most of us have ever known about that we are stunned to learn of the scope and magnitude of the torment. There is a woman who has a mother and father who married after the Holocaust. Previous to World War II, each of her parents had been married to other partners and each had children. This woman's parents each lost an entire family. After the war, they met and were married. This woman has immense guilt feelings when she considers the fact that were it not for the Holocaust, she might not have been born. To put it so very bluntly, had her father's first wife and her mother's first husband not ended up on a heap of bodies similar to the one shown here, she might not be alive to carry the burden of her existence. Indeed the psychological effects of the great atrocity are so unique, so incomprehensible in the main, that psychiatric assistance to the victims, both survivors and the children of survivors, is limited at best.

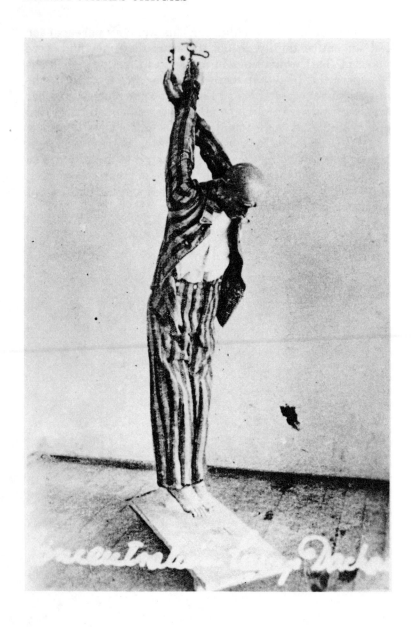

Yes, his feet are off the ground. And "yes" answers the question we each have about his shoulders too. There is nothing this man can do to in any manner alleviate the pain he is experiencing on this torture post at Dachau. How long he must hang we do not know. Sixty seconds would be excruciating and these punishments were often handed out for eight hour periods. Any kind of movement would increase this man's torment. If he fainted, chances were that some guard would revive him so that he might not escape the feeling of punishment. And what might have been the "crime" for which this man was punished? Maybe the shape of his nose offended someone. Possibly he complained about an aspect of camp life. Maybe, when someone else was being tortured and the prisoners were forced to witness the victim being made an example of, maybe this man averted his eyes out of compassion, shame, disgust, fear. Perhaps he stole a second cup of soup when one cup was meant to suffice for the entire day. At a certain point during this meat-hooking, this human being undoubtedly lost control of his bodily functions. We probably can't even imagine the condition he was in, if he survived this treatment. His arms would be almost function-less. He could not clean or feed himself for a very long time. Since he would not be able to work, and the authorities were unwilling to "carry" those people who did not earn their keep—that would be bad economics—this man's chances for living very much longer beyond the time he is seen here, are minimal. Did he know that he was photographed here? Did the photographer try to remain unobtrusive or did he tease the victim? "Hey, Jew, look-up, smile." A lot of people participated in the torture and death of a lot of people.

HARRY JAMES CARGAS

Bodies everywhere. Especially at the war's end you could hardly find an area of a camp which had no dead or dying persons. A look at the feet of these victims shows something of the conditions in which they lived. The shabby substitutes these men wore for shoes indicate how pathetic their clothing situation was. The calloused feet of those not fortunate enough to have even rags emphasize the problem. From such piles of bodies will the European Jewish culture ever rise again? The Yiddish language is close to extinction because so many who spoke it perished in the Holocaust. A companion question is this: Will European Christian culture flourish again? Christian Europe was the scene in which the great tragedy took place. People today speak of a post-Christian Europe existing now. Is that true? We who are Christians are staggered by the magnitude of the moral crimes committed in World War II. Did God die at Auschwitz? Can there be some kind of resurrection if the Christian believes that somehow God did abandon us? We have to be careful not to make theological games of such questions. They are much too important for that. But we can be certain of this: if Christianity is to be relevant today, it will have to prove itself by confronting the roles that Christians played in the persecution, humiliation, torture and murder of the people some have labelled Christ killers. For the Christians, Christ was killed 12,000,000 times at Birkenau, Dachau, Auschwitz, Majdanek and the other camps, many by people who said that they themselves were Christians. Calling myself a follower of Jesus does not make it so. Only in trying to act like Jesus will this be so. This is the Jesus who suffered rather than caused pain; who did penance in the face of temptations; who spoke of love of all humanity. How has that image been corrupted?

151

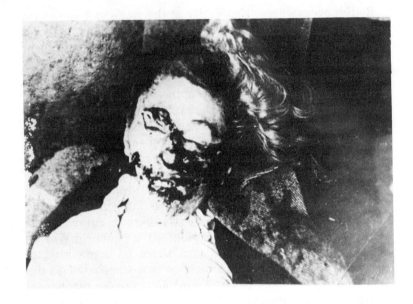

Badly beaten people like this one at Lodz were commonly seen in the camps. In the thirteenth century, St. Thomas Aquinas wrote that we cannot love what we do not know. But today we ask, "How can we hate persons whom we do not know?" Chaim Kaplan, one who did not outlive the Holocaust but whose *Scroll of Agony* did, posed this very question. "After all," Kaplan noted of one of the many terrifying incidents, "the victim was a stranger, not an old enemy; he did not speak rudely to him (the aggressor), let alone touch him. Then why this cruel wrath! How is it possible to attack a stranger to me, a man of flesh and blood like myself, to wound him and trample upon him, and cover his body with sores, bruises, and welts, without any reason?" What could this woman shown here have done to warrant such a beating? How offensive could she have been to someone who was physically more powerful than she? Possibly she was merely trying to defend a friend, a relative, a child of hers from harm. If so, she was acting normally; but her treatment in return was far from normal. The blood clotted face is almost like a map of persecution. The woman's obviously beautiful hair, flowing behind her, no doubt was used as a frame to highlight what was perhaps a quite lovely face. She was no doubt the pride of some man in her appearance; she may have made a number of men's hearts pound a little differently than usual when she walked by because of her physical charm. But now she cannot be concerned with her appearance. We can guess that only pain and survival are matters for attention. Is she aware that she is now being photographed? If she is, then she must also know the reason she is the object of interest: not because she is lovely to look at but rather because she looks horrible. She is right at this instant reduced to a symbol of the might of the Third Reich. Nothing, no one, must stand in the way of the Nazi will.

It's not only the humiliation of a man, mocking him and his religious beliefs, that catches our attention. It's also the obvious glee with which this is being done. Just look at the happy faces of the soldiers as they make sport of a man who's dignity seems to be holding up through this episode. The troops are pleased with themselves, clearly. They were perhaps fortified by the slogan, rampant in Germany for so many years previous to the Second World War: "Hep! Hep! Hep! Death and destruction to all Jews." (Not *death* alone, but somehow *destruction* as well. Destruction of their sense of humanity?) And there was the other motto: "The Jews are our misfortune." The Nazis regularly chanted, "Germany wake up, Judah drop dead." During the middle 1920's, it is estimated that over 700 racist, anti-Judaic newspapers were published throughout Germany. It is in one of these, the SA organ *Sturmlied,* that these words were published: "And when Jewish blood spurts from the knife, things will go twice as well." The men taking part in this "initiation ceremony" are all officers. While two are actively clipping locks emblematic of religious conviction, the others are apparently less interested in what is going on than in posing for the cameraman. The man second from the right certainly wants to look as handsome as he can for immortality. The tallest man went to the back of the group so as not to block out any of the others. A thoughtful man. This, by the way, is only one of a series of photographs in which this particular Jew is the center of attraction. How long did his agony last? How long did it take to set up each of these shots? How many pictures were taken that are lost? Did the photographer promise copies of the photo to each of the officers? Did he make a good profit from the occasion? Or good contacts for future work?

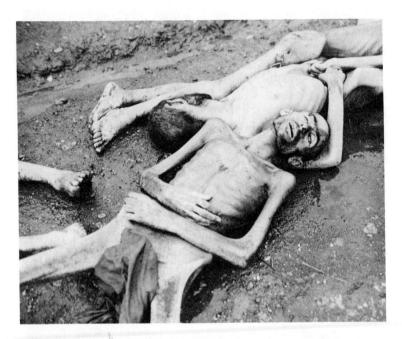

Looking at massive piles of bodies of Holocaust victims may be like reading books of history about the events. The statistics are appalling but they sometimes appeal most exclusively to the intellect, which is interested in the nature of facts. Seeing individual corpses may be more like reading a novel about the Holocaust wherein it is our emotions which are more moved. Here we have a photograph which might evoke a variety of emotions: sorrow, horror, disgust, pity, possibly despair. We may speculate on the victim and the photographer. Perhaps both suffered in different ways. The dead man's body is emaciated. It is evident that he did not die quickly. Rather his was an extended agony. We need only to look at his hips to come to some understanding of the degree of starvation to which he was subject. Perhaps that was the cause of his death. A long look at this man's face will prove of itself a profound homily on the Holocaust. The photographer may have undergone a certain amount of pain, too, although

156

of a less final kind. It may have been he, out of a sense of compassion, who covered the man's penis to keep him from a kind of posthumous shame. The cameraman is no doubt standing in the midst of bodies, having to be careful where he steps, perhaps fearful of tripping and falling onto the ground among the cadavers. No doubt he selected this victim as a subject because he was face up and because of that sermon on his face. We might try to reconstruct a career, a biography, for the man shown here in the Laudsberg concentration camp but fiction ought more properly be about fictional characters. This man was real, his pain was real and we will not intrude on that reality. Rather, let us allow him to intrude on our reality. Let us thus respond to his death rather than ignore it and thereby risk ignoring our own humanity.

In one way, the man in this photograph is fortunate. He was allowed to go to the toilet. Often prisoners in the concentration camps, while never permitted to go to the bathroom during twelve hour work days, would not be allowed to use the facilities at night either, if the whims of the guards so dictated. We know from the work of writers like Terrence Des Pres and others that for long periods of time inmates would be covered with their own filth, or that of others given the bunk bed arrangements in which they slept. But while the man here is in one way lucky, his is not an enviable condition. Humiliation never is. No doubt he has seen the cameraman approach. The photograph looks like it had benefit of a flashbulb, so the prisoner knew at some point that he was being mocked. He is trying to maintain anonymity here at the trough, a trough the type of which some Jews were actually drowned in because some *kapo* or guard decided that humanity would be better off that way. Privacy of any kind was denied such prisoners as this man. In many instances, so was paper by which men and women might clean themselves. These people, rabbis, teachers, laborers, clerks, musicians, dressmakers, remained very dirty; they smelled. Some therefore hated each other and soon hated themselves. They were systematically degraded by not only their conquerors but others who were also conquered by the Nazis yet who joined in league with Nazis to destroy Jews. Auschwitz, Buchenwald, Dachau, Treblinka, Sobibor and the other infamous camps were each an entire hell thrust on people who deserved only to live lives of decency, respect, love, creativity and whatever normalcy means.

Often a Jew walking down the street was simply picked up by the authorities and never seen by his family again. Maybe this man was just such a victim. After the disappearance of a day or so his wife and children would have to fully recognize that the sick feelings in their stomachs were there because the man of their family was just poof, gone. The odds were great that he would never return. We know that in the days before very sophisticated cameras were engineered, no one could move when a shot was being taken or the film would be blurred. Hence we can deduce that this photo was "posed." The main figure in this scene was obviously forced to stand while the picture taker "got it all together." Maybe this Jew

was moved around to take advantage of the right light for this shot. But his thoughts are only tangentially on the photographer. He is miles away. Where? With a family somewhere? With an ailing brother elsewhere in the camp? With a child murdered by Nazis? With a God whose tolerance of evil puzzles him? The possibilities are enormous. Was this a face that ever laughed, told jokes, wrinkled up in playful attitude for a loved one? Did these eyes ever sparkle, show insight, compassion, understanding? Is he now vowing revenge, despairing, plotting, going mad? This emaciated man, weighed down by a couple of bags, has the kind of look that is capable of haunting a viewer for a long time. What is in those bags, by the way? Not pistols and ammunition, not slabs of meat or packages of fresh fruit. Not cash, not a change of clothing. We will never know—but we can be sure that, as the world judges value during normal times, whatever this man was allowed to carry could not have been deemed to be of even small value. But that's irrelevant. For us, now, it's the look on his face which matters.

These bodies are tied at the feet for convenience. For convenience. Words attached to this U.S. Army documentation photograph indicate that this is a scene, a close-up of a grave, in a German camp identified as Lager #3. The corpses are stacked five high in mass graves approximately 12 feet by 50. The victims, we read, are French, Russian and Polish Jews who died from starvation, typhus or poison injected by hypodermic needles. This particular pit is estimated to hold 1,000 bodies. The quotation closes with this unembellished statement: "There were many such pits in the camp." What can we think in the face of such facts? We who are used to expending our pity on "ordinary" deaths, or those who suffer broken limbs, or some who are beaten on the stock market, or

a friend who flunked a test, how do we express emotion over a tragedy of such magnitude? We can't be blamed, can we, for not knowing how to feel, what to feel? A certain kind of overwhelming numbness may be all that we can experience. Tied at the feet for what?—convenience? Convenience? What mattered here was the convenience of the criminals. The victims were beneath any consideration. Often ruthless Nazis were observed showing acts of kindness to animals, indicating an apparent sincerity of attitude. How was such compassion deflected from a whole set of human beings? How is it so very many easily cooperated in Hitler's scheme of annihilation? We cannot but be obsessed by the possibility that we too might have fallen into the moral abyss of complicity as an easy way out. Would we just follow orders as so many at war crime trials said in their defense that they did? If there is to be a final Judgment Day, do we think such an excuse will hold up before the God in whose image and likeness we are said to be created; in whose image and likeness the victims are said to have been created also?

It was German practice to photograph violence done against Jews in other countries and publish such pictures to prove how universal the hatred of Jews had become. Here is an exemplary scene with a photograph including another photographer in his record. How eager some were to try to immortalize particular events. Note the fact that these are portable gallows, capable of being moved to various locations for the benefit of maximum attendance. Here is a way of showcasing Nazi policies, Nazi justice. And as we can see sketchily, there was a large crowd witnessing the public executions in Lodz, Poland. The expression on the young soldier's face is far more serious, more thoughtful, than the smiles we have found on the faces of other troops who were themselves guilty of war crimes. Was this near-lad the executioner? Or is he here to guard the bodies so that the wives and children of the victims can't cut them down for decent burial? Why have the people who make up the crowd come to observe the hangings? Are they so fascinated by the event, so eager to see the instant that is universally feared? Or are these townspeople forced to witness the executions, forced to see three men made an example of? We cannot even begin to speculate on the reasons for which these men were condemned. They may have been saboteurs, black marketeers, Jews, hostages, reprisal victims, political enemies, kin of a wanted enemy—there is no way of our telling. We do know that all of the above qualified one for the gallows. So did the stealing of food to feed one's children; so did listening to a secret radio; so did disrespectfully addressing a Nazi officer; so did ... Whim, just the whim of a Nazi could condemn a Jew or Gypsy or other foe of the Third Reich to instant death—or prolonged dying. Depending on the way a hangman ties a noose, one can die quickly or very slowly on the gallows. The executioner is, alas, one of the symbols that may be applied to this century.

In a 1950 film titled *The Gunfighter*, Gregory Peck plays a kind of sympathetic outlaw whose reputation as the "fastest gun" lures men into trying to outdraw him so that they can gain fame for shooting down the legendary figure. Early in the film, an older, obviously incompetent man, tries to kill

Johnny Ringo (Peck) because the man mistakenly thinks that Ringo killed his son. When Ringo disarms the would be avenging father, and claims innocence of the boy's murder, the unbelieving elderly cowboy says that Ringo probably has forgotten the incident. Ringo responds with words something like this: "You never forget a man you kill." That seems like such a truism. But mass destruction of human beings shows how empty such a statement can be. Nowhere is this more true than in the Nazi atrocities. It is very likely, given what we know of the attempted annihilation of the Jews, that all of the bodies pictured in this photograph from Latvia fell before one executioner. Surely this man, like the many multiple murderers of World War II, did not remember all of his victims. To him, these were not men and women and children; these were vermin, individual pestilences. He knew them no more than we know termites or water bugs that we try to stamp out in large numbers. Generally, even when we do exterminate such pests, we do not do so in such large quantities as did the Nazi destroyers and their collaborators. The numbers of bodies in this, as in so many photographic documents that exist, are uncountable. Piled on top of each other so randomly and quantitatively they are like a tiny Milky Way when seen through a telescope—so undistinguishable because so disorderly great in number. What we see here is not even an hour's "work," and the soldiers worked very long hours we know.

However we define Hope, we see here a man who has none. His anguish is not superficial; it has penetrated his soul. To speculate on the cause of this victim's condition might be to dishonor him. But we may wonder if he survived the moment. His pain seems too complete, so overwhelming that this may have been the final expression of his life. Jewish psychiatrists who themselves had concentration camp experiences have written about how some (of the few) who survived the death

camps were able to do so. Bruno Bettelheim suggests that
certain men and women took on the personality of their
aggressors in order to get through alive. Leo Eitinger, after
having analyzed many patients who, like himself, barely
outlived Auschwitz and other camps, feels that one, almost
indispensable element to the survival of many, was having a
close relative sharing the atrocity experiences. Those who lost
their entire families or who were separated from them in a
kind of absolute way did not have this opportunity. Viktor
Frankl, the founder of logotherapy, a psychiatric approach
based on hope—the hope of being reunited with a loved one, of
completing a particular project—saw this as being important
to a relatively large number of survivors. But the man in this
photograph seems to have none of these. His posture is hardly
of one who is aggressive in any form. Furthermore, here he
seems so alone that abandonment by family, friends, even
God, appears to be reflected in his cry. And it is despair, not
hope, which is reflected in his face, a despair which may have
come from a realization that he is a creature suspended on

165

earth, with ties to no one, no thing. Nor are we taking into account any physical pain this person is suffering. How cold is he? How long has it been since he has eaten? Is disease ravaging his body the way it did nearly all who lived for any length of time in the death camps? In a culture saturated with the false emotions of Hollywood, television soap operas, advertisers, self-pitiers and sycophants in general, can we long contemplate the true emotion of this miserable, miserable human being? We must.

IV
TOWARDS RECONCILIATION

In 1944, as the Second World War was nearing its end, a papal nuncio is reported to have said this: "There is no innocent blood of Jewish children in the world. All Jewish blood is guilty. You have to die. This is the punishment that has been awaiting you because of [deicide]."[1]

To a survivor of the Holocaust, the perspective is quite different. Alexander Donat in *The Holocaust Kingdom* says that this question was raised in the death camp: "How can Christianity survive the discovery that after a thousand years of its being Europe's official religion, Europe remains pagan at heart?" (New York, 1965), pp. 230-231.

Contemporary literature, the great barometer of the pressures of the subconscious, raises that question in perhaps an even more fundamental way. What is reality? We need only to read the novels of Alain Robbe-Grillet, Nathalie Sarraute, Carlos Fuentes, Gabriel Garcia Marques, Raymond Queneau, Kurt Vonnegut, Samuel Beckett, Severo Sarduy, and many others, from nations which have been identified as Christian, to know that the questions about the meaning of existence are being asked again because the pre-Auschwitz and pre-Buchenwald pat answers we had went up in the flames of ovens which were prepared for Jews and others.

Questioning, of course, is an absolute necessity today. As a friend told the young Elie Wiesel, just before Wiesel was to be shipped to a death camp: "I pray to the God within me that He will give me the strength to ask Him the right questions" (*Night*, p. 16). Novelists and philosophers known as the Absurdists ask questions from despair. This seems appropriate for those in the class of persecutors. What is amazing is that the victims—the Jews—are mainly able to ask their questions in a framework of hope.

However, this hope has its roots in experience and is not a naive, childish desire. I heard someone ask Wiesel if he believed in God. His reply should be made known to all Christians. "If I told you that I believe in God, I would be lying; if I told you that I did not believe in God, I would be lying. If I told you that I believe in man, I would be lying; if I told you I did not believe in man, I would be lying. But one thing I do know: the Messiah has not come yet." In *The Crucifixion of the Jews*, Protestant theologian Franklin H. Littell has written this, from his Christian perspective:

> The truth about the murder of European Jewry by baptized Christians is this: it raises in a most fundamental way the question of the credibility of Christianity. Was Jesus a false messiah? No one can be a true messiah whose followers feel compelled to torture and destroy other human persons who think differently. Is the Jewish people, after all and in spite of two millennia of Christian calumny, the true Suffering Servant promised in Isaiah? (p. 16).

Littell has observed, it was noted earlier, that if Christ and Peter and Paul had lived during the Nazi period, they would have perished at Auschwitz. We may be forgiven for asking if maybe they did. Perhaps these deaths were, in a sense preparatory to a resurrection in a meaningful, spiritual sense. Christianity, as an ideal, has been less than inspiringly visible. The Christianity of the Cross may have been present, in a large part, only ironically in history. J. Coert Rylarsdaam saw that if being a Christian meant the taking up of the Cross, and being crucified for God, then the only practicing Christians are the Jews![2] Russian thinker Nicolas Berdyaev would have agreed: "Perhaps the saddest thing to admit is that those who rejected the Cross have to carry it, while those who welcomed it are as often engaged in crucifying others."[3]

It is clear that we Christians may not hide behind the heroics of Franz Jagersdatter, Alfred Delp, and the relatively few others who identified evil as evil, refused to rationalize or compromise with it, and died as martyrs in Hitler's time. We may not take for granted that we would have been numbered with them had the opportunity arisen. If Original Sin includes us, so does Auschwitz. In retaining the Bible while denying the people who are its subject, we Christians are guilty of arrogance. In declaring ourselves the people of the New Israel, we are guilty of arrogance.

A serious ecumenism must be attempted, on a level far higher than what we are experiencing currently. I've personally lived in over a dozen dioceses since the end of the war against the Jews and I've not noticed any extraordinary ecumenical effort on the part of official Catholicism—and Auschwitz requires extraordinary ecumenical effort. Most of what I can see is similar to a Russian Five Year Farm Plan. The right offices are established, the right papers are filled out with comforting figures, but at the end of the period, where is the grain?

Let me offer a series of points which I feel we, as Christians, might implement in order to bring us closer to our Jewish brothers and sisters, people we have violently alienated for so long. Basically, the suggestions are aimed at institutional actions rather than individual. This is intentional, because it would be presumptuous for one Christian to tell another how to best react to history. That will have to be a personal approach. But because we are all a part of the Church, in the way that we are, it is not only appropriate but imperative that we require of the Church certain acts in our name. It will take experts in various disciplines to more fully elaborate on each of the points below, but let me merely list them, then comment briefly on each for whatever value these suggestions may have:

1. The Catholic Church should excommunicate Adolf Hitler.
2. The Christian liturgical calendar(s) should include an annual memorial service for Jewish victims of the Holocaust.
3. We Christians must publicly and officially admit the errors of our teachers where they were wrong concerning Jews.
4. The Christian Church must insist on the essential Jewishness of Christianity.
5. Jesus should be recognized as a link between Jews and Christians.
6. The church's teachings on the subject of evil need to be re-evaluated.
7. Traditional Christian theologies of history must be re-examined.
8. The Vatican historical archives for the twentieth century need to be opened to historians.
9. Chairs of Judaic Studies ought to be established at more Christian colleges and universities.
10. We might look to see if a redefinition of the notion of inspiration in Christian scripture is appropriate.
11. Christians must find new terminology for what we now designate as the Old Testament and the New Testament.
12. Catholics must demand an encyclical letter which deals specifically with the sins of anti-Judaism and with the sins of Christians in their actions toward Jews.
13. The heavy Christian emphasis on missionizing should be redirected toward perfecting indivi-

dual Christian lives.

14. We Christians need to get on our knees and repent our sins against Jewish people.

Undoubtedly this list should be considerably larger and readers may wish to add points for consideration. However, these fourteen, important as I see them, are offered for starters at least. Each deserves some elaboration.

1. *The Catholic Church should excommunicate Adolf Hitler.* Excommunication is, we know, a punishment meted out by the official Church to living persons whose conduct is considered to be scandalous from a Christian moral viewpoint. Hence there has been no purpose, traditionally, for imposing such a penalty on a dead person. But I think that we need to show our Jewish friends that with this belated act we are serious about developing ecumenical interaction with Jews. Hitler died a member in good standing with Rome. Jews know that and find the fact incredible. So do Christians who are made aware. Women and men have been denied participation in the church's sacraments for *comparatively* trivial acts: divorce and remarriage, stealing papal property, dueling, voting for the Communist Party in Italy—it has even been threatened against certain contemporary priests who have persisted in saying the mass in Latin. But Hitler somehow did not qualify! Posthumous excommunication would not only be an ecumenical sign, it would also show today's neo-Nazis that their anti-Jewish activities will not be tolerated by the Catholic Church.

2. *The Christian liturgical calendar(s) should include an annual memorial service for Jewish victims of the Holocaust.* This will not only indicate to the Jewish community that a new spirit is emerging, it will also help to energize Christian consciences about the awe-ful

event. Germany's Catholic novelist Gunter Grass has written that "What is asked of us is to understand Auschwitz in its historical past, recognize it in the present, and not assume blindly that Auschwitz lies behind us."⁴ I suggest that one important way to remember the Holocaust in all of its significance is through liturgical memorialization on a regular basis. Preachers would be thus encouraged to discuss its implications and congregations would be awakened to them.

3. *We as Christians must publicly and officially admit the errors of our teachers where they were wrong concerning Jews.* This will be a long time, ongoing process. It would be ludicrous, after over 1500 years of calumny toward Jews (or at best of official silence where holy words were necessary), to simply say we're sorry and then to expect the scales to be thus balanced. Christianity has never properly been seen as a religion in which scales are to be equalized. Sanctity—that is the striving for rather than achievement of perfection— requires an overbalance, not a this for that. And if we are to achieve such a "weight" in regard to our relations with Jews, then it is obvious that it will take a very long and very intensive effort. Certain statements of St. John Chrysostom and St. Justin and St. Cyprian and St. Hippolytus and St. Bernard of Clairvaux and the all star list of anti-Judaists must be contradicted so that the world will know that we abjure these words. It is not enough that this theologian or that writer or a particular bishop say the necessary things. But officially, popes and patriarchs and bishops' councils and pastors in the pulpit, in their parish bulletins, in the diocesan newspapers and everywhere else appropriate begin and continue to teach the love of Jews.

4. *The Christian church must insist on the essential*

Jewishness of Christianity. This point will need elaboration only to the theologically retarded. And yet it is necessary for us to consider the harm that anti-Judaism does to Christians at the same time that we discuss the victimization of Jews. Every anti-Judaist is a slave—a slave to hatred of a particular kind. Dr. Martin Luther King, Jr., seriously cared about the effect of racism on the racist. He knew that the psychological danger to the person who hates may in the longer view, be far more disastrous to *that* person's group, to the persecutor's group, than to the people being tormented. What has happened to the Christian psyche over the centuries? How have we withstood the boomerang assault of anti-Judaism? How can we square St. Paul's teaching on the greatness of charity while supporting—at least by our silence—exile, ghettoization, imprisonment, torture, and murder of Jews?

5. *Jesus should be recognized as a link between Jews and Christians.* This point is a logical derivative of the previous one, on the essential Jewishness of Christianity. Too often Jesus has been offered as a stumbling block between Christians and Jews, as a rationale for mutual exclusion. Here is an excerpt from a document written under the sponsorship of the Commission on Faith and Order of the National Council of Churches and the Secretariat for Catholic-Jewish Relations of the National Conference for Catholic Bishops: "The Church of Christ is rooted in the life of the People of Israel. We Christians look upon Abraham as our spiritual ancestor and father of our faith. . . . The ministry of Jesus and the life of the early Christian community were thoroughly rooted in the Judaism of their day, particularly in the teachings of the Pharisees. The Christian Church is still sustained by the living faith of the patriarchs and prophets, kings and priests, scribes and rabbis, and the

people whom God chose for his own. Christ is the link . . .
enabling the Gentiles to be numbered among Abraham's 'offspring' and therefore fellow-heirs with the
Jews according to God's promise. It is a tragedy of
history that Jesus, our bond of unity with the Jews, has
all too often become a symbol and source of division and
bitterness because of human weakness and pride."[5]
Tragedy of history indeed—for Jews, for Christians.

6. *The church's teachings on the subject of evil need to be
re-evaluated.* St. Thomas Aquinas has carried the
burden of traditional thinking on this subject. He
identified evil as nothing, no-thing, an absence of a good
or perfection. (We are here basically speaking of moral
evil which is equated with sin, rather than physical
evil—imperfections in nature such as earthquakes—or
metaphysical evil which is attributed to limitations due
to the finiteness of the human condition.) Carl Gustav
Jung has written convincingly on the psychological
need for each of us as individuals, and for collective
groups such as nations, to recognize the role of evil in
our natures and in our actions. Consideration of the
deaths of the six million Jews, and the deaths of the fifty
million in World War II, force us to inquire further as to
the nature of evil. It is possible that a key to a fuller
understanding on this topic will be found in the
movement popularly designated as process theology. To
caricaturize the teachings in process theology we might
say that it applies certain principles of evolution to
God's development. God is not static, God changes, and
part of that change is determined by our activities. If
this is true, perhaps the same is true of Satan as well. At
any rate, the possibilities for insight from process
thought seem very great and it needs to be studied.

7. *Traditional Christian theologies of history need to
be re-examined.* Generally, history has been regarded as

the unfolding plan of God for humanity; or as a *Weltanschauung* based on the providential action of God in human affairs. For many today, it is difficult to see how the Holocaust fits into such concepts. Karl Rahner, one of the most influential Christian thinkers of our era, says that many questions regarding the theology of history require considerable study. Among those he indicates are the purposive unity of human history, the theology of history before Christ, the sanctification of the entire sphere of the "profane" through the Christian church and much more, including the very basic problem of the theological meaning of a theology of history. Those of us who are nearly overwhelmed by Auschwitz feel a terrible inability to put its relevance into any pattern. Many feel it is outside of any overall plan. If true, that must be reflected in our analysis of the meaning of history.

8. *The Vatican historical archives for the twentieth century need to be opened to historians.* There are two aspects to this suggestion; one might be termed positive, the other negative. We might ask, what is the value gained by having Vatican documents unavailable to scholars? Are events of that period so shameful to the Catholic Church that they need to be hidden? That is certainly one conclusion being drawn by some people. It isn't enough for Vatican officials to make responses to criticism of church action and inaction during and just preceding the Nazi period. Such responses are of the "if you only had all of the facts, you'd see things in a more favorable light" variety. Well then, give us the facts. If Pius XII's reputation is being besmirched because of ignorance based only on speculation, let us have the rest of the story. Rolf Hochhuth's drama *The Deputy* was scorned by certain churchmen in its emphasis on Pius XII's inaction on behalf of Jews. But the suspicions of

the rest of us who "don't have the full picture" are not put to rest merely because some bishops say that they should be. What has Rome to hide? If little or nothing, we should know that so that the prestige of the papacy may be considerably restored. If there are, in fact, as many believe, monumental errors of judgment (to put it one way) which the archives will reveal, we must know that also. *All* of the facts need to be revealed. If it is found that the hierarchy of the church, in a sense acting for many of us, behaved immorally, that must be revealed and admissions must be made and, yes, penance must be begun. How can we correct past abuses unless we know them? Indeed we may be condemned to repeat these errors, as George Santayana would suggest, unless we recognize them as such. But we cannot know them fully if the Vatican, claiming a purpose of promulgating truth, in fact hides the truth. A second aspect of what some see as a Vatican coverup, what might be described as a silence after the Silence, is the right of certain persons to their good names. There are, we know, a number of Christians, relatively small yet not insignificant, who aided Jews during the decade 1935-1945. And some did so with great personal risk. There were those who lost their lives in this holy work. Their actions need to be made public not only for their sakes, but for ours as well. The rest of us are starving for stories of Christian heroes during this period. We are depressed, psychologically battered, by the contrary evidence. Our emotional balance requires more than what we have now in the knowledge of Christians actively being Christian on behalf of Jews. Undoubtedly there is evidence for this in the Vatican archives. Why is this, too, being suppressed?

9. *Chairs of Judaic Studies ought to be established at more Christian colleges and universities.* This has been

done at a few institutions around the world but if we are
to make a serious effort at learning about Judaism—and
in an important sense therefore learning about our
Christian heritage—such chairs of study are well
advised. Furthermore, they ought properly to be funded
by Christian groups rather than Jewish ones. Again, we
need to let the world in general, and Jewish women and
men in particular, know that we Christians are serious
in our attempts at coming closer to Jews in a very true
spiritual way. And perhaps it need not be said, yet
perhaps it does, that Jewish as well as Christian
scholars be appointed to such posts. In one of the recent
crises of growth in the United States, few recommended
that black studies programs be exclusively taught and
directed by white teachers and administrators on
campus. Men were not being asked to develop women's
academic programs. The analogy is obvious and,
ultimately, does warrant mention since for so long, at so
many schools, Jewish scripture and tradition was
taught exclusively by non-Jews. Perhaps there will
come a time when such an arrangement will be more
acceptable—both when Christians have become radically immersed in their pre-Jesus roots and when the
pains of persecutions of Jews are of historical memory
only—but this is not such a time, nor can we see it in the
near or, alas, even the reasonably remote future.

10. *We might look to see if a redefinition of the notion
of inspiration in Christian scripture is appropriate.*
Gregory Baum wrote this as a priest: "If the Church
wants to clear itself of the anti-Jewish trends built into
its teaching, a few marginal correctives will not do. It
must examine the very center of its proclamation and
reinterpret the meaning of the gospel for our times."[6]
He presses further and insists that "What the encounter
of Auschwitz demands of Christian theologians, there-

fore, is that they submit Christian teaching to a radical ideological critique."[7] Some Christian theologians admit of no anti-Jewish bias in their Bible but that seems indefensible today. Others see this bias but maintain that this comes not from inspiration, but by interpolation of early Christians to meet certain contemporary exegeses. An eloquent current voice on this subject is Rosemary Radford Ruether whose book *Faith and Fatricide* has caused many to ask for a more complete exploration of Christian teachings on biblical inspiration. To quote Baum once again, ". . . what if God is addressing the Church anew through the awful event of the holocaust?"[8] Ruether and others are asking the same question. We can ignore it on no level, including the level of scripture study.

11. *Christians must find new terminology for what we now designate as the Old Testament and the New Testament.* Most Christians do not seem to be aware of how insulting these titles can be to Jews. At the very least, we can be seen as arrogant in implying by these names that "we" have appropriated "their" Book, updated it, fulfilled it and somehow have cornered the market on interpreting that earlier body of work. Indeed many, many Christian theologians, when writing on Genesis, Leviticus, Isaiah, never even consult Jewish commentators regarding exegeses of these works. In writing about pre-Christian biblical texts, father John Pawlikowski, who chairs the department of historical and doctrinal studies at Catholic Theological Union in Chicago, had this to say in *The National Catholic Reporter*:

> At best we see them as a prelude to the fullness of teaching found in the New Testament, not as containing religious insights vital in their own right. At worst, the term [Old Testament] allows the church to totally ignore

the rich spirituality found in these writings and to
continue to parrot the totally discredited notion of
Christianity as the religion of love in contrast to
Judaism's dependence on legalism. (April 21, 1978), p.
11.

Later Pawlikowski suggests that the term New Testament might be replaced by the designation "Apostolic
writings," originally offered by Dr. Eugene Fisher,
Director of the National Conference of Catholic Bishop's
Secretariat for Catholic-Jewish Relations. The term
Hebrew Scriptures, Pawlikowski notes further, "forces
upon us a recognition of Judaism as a separate religious
tradition whose Scriptures we share but do not own."
There are problems here, including the fact that the
pre-Christian scriptures for Roman Catholics include
certain Greek works which are not a part of the Hebrew
canon and I am not insisting on any particular new
name for what is now referred to as the Old Testament.
But I am urging a change of title which Jews will find
acceptable and which will be, in an important sense,
truer.

12. *Catholics must demand an encyclical letter which
deals specifically with the sins of anti-Judaism and with
the sins of Christians in their actions towards Jews.* In
the second chapter of this book, a written but unpublished encyclical on this subject was briefly discussed.
Pope Pius XI had commissioned such a letter but died
(under suspicious circumstances) and it is believed by
many that the publication of the encyclical would have
had an important effect on the prosecution of the
program of annihilation of the Jews which was implemented so forcefully not long after Pius XI's death. It is
well known that when Christianity, speaking through
certain church officials, objected to the implementation
of Hitler's euthanasia plan (which was to put to death

"unproductive" citizens—the aged, the retarded, the terminally ill, for example) the Germans quickly reacted by almost totally eliminating the practice. It is not too much to believe that a strong reaction by Rome to anti-Judaism as it was raging at the time would have had important consequences for all humanity. Pius XI's document concluded by urging all of the world's Catholic clergy to work against anti-Judaism (and racism) everywhere. In the unpublished letter we read that no totalitarian government by its nature can understand the concept of the Common Good. It can be observed that in such governments, "no hesitation is felt at simply stripping men of their liberty and still less hesitation at violating the sanctity of house and home." We read later that "the very essence of the State [is] to recognize in all men an equal right to life; a recognition which cannot be avoided and a right to be protected by law." And then the document becomes hard hitting: "The theory and practice of racism which makes a distinction between the higher and lower races, ignores the bond of unity . . ." And later, and more specifically (for our purposes here), the letter makes reference to the Nuremberg Laws, whose bases were totally anti-Judaic: "What a fearful insult to a race and what a degradation of humanity when marriage between the members of different racial groups is systematically prohibited . . . It is further increased when it becomes clear that the struggle for racial purity ends by becoming uniquely the struggle against the Jews." And for a final quotation from this much needed work: In reponse to anti-Judaism, "the answer of the church is unequivocal and unchanging. Her answer is determined by no earthly policy, but by her fidelity to the truth bequeathed to her custody by her Divine Founder . . . it established a universal Kingdom, in which there would be no

distinction of Jew or Gentile, Greek or barbarian . . .
These same doctrines likewise show the utter unfitness
and inefficacy of anti-Semitism." As Michael Mashberg,
writing in *The National Jewish Monthly* (April, 1978),
p. 46, has judged: "If the Vatican chooses not to publish
[this encyclical] as an historical document and make
known the circumstances surrounding Pius XII's attitude toward the encyclical, then, the silence of the
Vatican will increase the din of its critics and magnify
Pope Pius XII's refusal to issue a condemnation of Nazi
racial policies." In an important way, Christians too
have been failed by the non-publication of the treatise.
We must demand that it be made public, or a letter
expressly like it, and that it be given official church
endorsement.

13. *The heavy Christian emphasis on missionizing
should be redirected toward perfecting individual Christian lives.* Missionary efforts, however well intentioned,
are generally not as well received by the presumed
beneficiaries as they are enthusiastically endorsed by
those of the performing group. Perhaps Christians
might comprehend this better if they tried to imagine
how they would react if Jews tried to convert us to
Judaism. The true missionary activity, we must realize,
is in the perfection of our individual, personal lives. If
what we do, if how we live, is worthy of emulation, that
will be missionary activity enough. An example in the
right direction may be seen in the work of the
Congregation of Notre Dame De Sion, founded in
France in 1846. This religious order was begun by two
brothers, Marie Alphonse and Marie Theodore Ratis-
bonne, Catholic converts from Judaism, with avowed
aims to bring about a better understanding between
Christians and Jews and for the conversion of the latter.
Now, however, the women and men who are followers of

the Ratisbonnes (the men's group is called the Fathers of Sion) insist that proselytizing must be completely abandoned and they are leaders in what are efforts in what is described as Christian-Jewish dialogue.

14. *We Christians need to get on our knees and repent our sins against the Jewish people.* I mean the Jews of history: past, present, yes, future Jews too. They must all understand that we know of our errors and that we have a collective (and individual) firm purpose of amendment. One way to prove this, of course, will be, when we get off of our knees, to work for some of the suggestions made above, and for other ideas which will be developed by informed persons. However, as we approach our Jewish friends with suggestions, with plans, and in dialogue, we must do so in the spirit which Irving Greenberg demands of us: "Let us offer this fundamental criterion after the Holocaust. No statement, theological or otherwise, should be made that would not be credible in the presence of burning children."[9]

NOTES

Chapter I: Centuries of Christian Persecution of the Jews

[1]In Michael B. McGarry, *Christology After Auschwitz* (New York, 1977), p. 7.

[2]Quoted by Irving Greenberg in "Judaism and Christianity after the Holocaust" in *Journal of Ecumenical Studies*, XII (Fall, 1975), p. 526.

[3]McGarry, p. 4.

[4]Robert E. Willis, "Christian Theology after Auschwitz," *Journal of Ecumenical Studies*, XII (Fall, 1975), p. 495.

Chapter II: The Nazi Atrocities

[1]In Eva Fleischner, ed., *Auschwitz: Beginning of a New Era?* (New York, 1977), p. 8.

[2]Peter Viereck, *Metapolitics* (New York, 1961), p. 289.

[3]*Encyclopedia of the Third Reich* (New York, 1976), p. 252.

[4]*Harry James Cargas in Conversation with Elie Wiesel* (New York, 1976), pp. 40-42.

Chapter III: Towards Reconciliation

[1]Greenberg, pp. 525-526.

[2]*Ibid.*, p. 541.

[3]*Christianity and Anti-Semitism*, (Kent, 1952), p. 12.

[4]Quoted in Eva Fleischner, *Judaism in German Christian Theology Since 1945* (Metuchen, N.J., 1975), p. 21.

[5]McGarry, pp. 57-58.

[6]In his Introduction to Rosemary Radford Ruether, *Faith and Fatricide* (New York, 1974), pp. 6-7.

[7]*Ibid.*, p. 7.

[8]*Ibid.*, p. 8.

[9]Fleischner, p. 23.

BIBLIOGRAPHY

While my text draws most heavily on the work of Edward Flannery and Nora Levin for historical material, most of the entries in this bibliography have proven helpful to me at least to a certain degree. I have listed only books here. Anyone wishing for a broader bibliography, including periodical references, may wish to consult my reference volume *The Holocaust: An Annotated Bibliography* published by Catholic Library World (1977). In it, 425 books and articles are briefly described. Even though that publication is somewhat dated, it will still be of value to the serious student. The following bibliography draws heavily on my previous work but also contains references through 1980. Of course, I do not list every possible entry. William Styron's *Sophie's Choice* is not to be recommended as a work about the Holocaust; the writings of Bruno Bettelheim on the subject seem to me to be more self serving than authoritative, etc. These are personal decisions, based on whatever reading experience, knowledge and taste I have been able to acquire in more than a decade of study.

Abel, Theodore. *The Nazi Movement.* Atherton, 1966.

Aichinger, Ilse. *Herod's Children.* Atheneum, 1963.

Ainsztein, Reuben. *Jewish Resistance in Nazi Occupied Eastern Europe.* Barnes and Noble, 1975.

Allen, William Sheridan. *The Nazi Seizure of Power.* New Viewpoints, 1965.

Amery, Jean. *At the Mind's Limit.* Indiana University, 1980.

Andersch, Alfred. *Efrain's Book.* Doubleday, 1970.

Apenszlak, Jacob, (ed.). *The Black Book of Polish Jewry.* The American Federation for Polish Jews, 1943.

Arendt, Hannah. *Eichmann in Jerusalem.* Viking, 1964.

———— *The Origins of Totalitarianism.* World, 1958.

Arnold, Elliott. *A Night of Watching.* Fawcett, 1967.

HARRY JAMES CARGAS

Barkai, Meyer, (ed.). *The Fighting Ghettos.* Lippincott, 1962.

Bartoszewski, Sladyslaw. *The Samaritans.* Twayne, 1970.

Bauer, Yehuda. *The Holocaust in Perspective.* University of Washington, 1978.

Baumont, Maurice, John H.E. Fried and Edmond Vermeil, (eds.). *The Third Reich.* Praeger, 1955.

Becker, Jurek. *Jacob the Liar.* Harcourt Brace Jovanovich, 1975.

Beradt, Charlotte. *The Third Reich of Dreams.* Quadrangle, 1968.

Berg, Mary. *Warsaw Ghetto—A Diary.* L.B. Fisher, 1945.

Berkovitz, Eliezer. *Faith After the Holocaust.* KTAV, 1973.

Bertelsen, Aage. *October '43.* Putnam, 1954.

Birenbaum, Halina. *Hope Is the Last to Die.* Twayne, 1971.

Blagowidow, George. *The Last Train from Berlin.* Doubleday, 1977.

Boehm, Eric H., (ed.). *We Survived.* Yale University Press, 1949.

Boelcke, Willi A. *The Secret Conferences of Dr. Goebbels.* Dutton, 1970.

Bor, Josef. *Terezin Requiem.* Knopf, 1963.

Borowski, Tadeusz. *This Way for the Gas, Ladies and Gentlemen.* Viking, 1967.

Bosch, William J. *Judgement at Nuremberg.* University of North Carolina Press, 1970.

Braham, Randolph L. *The Politics of Genocide,* (two volumes). Columbia University, 1981.

Bramsted, Ernest K. *Goebbels and Nationalist Socialist Propaganda.* Michigan State University Press, 1965.

Brand, Joel, *Desperate Mission.* Criterion, 1958.

Brenner, Reeve Robert. *The Faith and Doubt of Holocaust Survivors.* Free Press, 1980.

Bullock, Alan. *Hitler: A Study in Tyranny.* Harper and Row, 1964.

Cargas, Harry James. *Harry James Cargas in Conversation with Elie Wiesel.* Paulist Press, 1976.

Chary, Frederick B. *The Bulgarian Jews and the Final Solution, 1940-1944.* University of Pittsburgh Press, 1972.

Cohen, Arthur A. *Arguments and Doctrines.* Harper and Row, 1970.

Cohen, Elie A. *The Abyss.* Norton, 1973.

_____ *Human Behavior in the Concentration Camp.* Norton, 1953.

Comer, Clarke. *Eichmann: The Man and His Crimes.* Ballantine, 1960.

Conway, John. *The Nazi Persecution of the Churches.* Macmillan, 1969.

Crankshaw, Edward. *The Gestapo: Instrument of Tyranny.* Viking, 1956.

Davidson, Eugene. *The Trial of the Germans.* Macmillan, 1966.

Dawidowicz, Lucy S., (ed.). *A Holocaust Reader.* Behrman House, 1976.

_____ *The War Against the Jews 1933-1945.* Holt, Rinehart and Winston, 1975.

Delbo, Charlotte. *None of Us Will Return.* Beacon, 1978.

D'Harcourt, Pierre. *The Real Enemy.* Scribner's, 1967.

Delarue, Jacques. *The Gestapo: A History of Horror.* Morrow, 1964.

DesPres, Terrence. *The Survivor.* Oxford, 1976.

Donat, Alexander. *The Holocaust Kingdom: A Memoir.* Holt, Rinehart, and Winston, 1965.

Dribben, Judith Strick. *A Girl Called Judith Strick.* Cowles, 1970.

Eckardt, A. Roy. *Elder and Younger Brothers*. Scribner's, 1967.

Edelman, Marek. *The Ghetto Fights*. American Representation of the General Jewish Workers' Union of Poland, 1946.

Eisner, Jack. *The Survivor*. Morrow, 1980.

Elkins, Michael, *Forged in Fury*. Ballantine, 1971.

Fackenheim, Emil. *God's Presence in History*. New York University Press, 1970.

Falconi, Carlo. *The Silence of Pius XII*. Little Brown, 1970.

Feingold, Henry. *The Politics of Rescue*. Rutgers University Press, 1970.

Fenelon, Fania. *Playing For Time*. Atheneum, 1977.

Ferdeber-Salz, Bertha. *And the Sun Kept Shining . . .* Schocken. 1980.

Fest, Joachim. *Adolph Hitler*. Harcourt Brace Jovanovich, 1974.

———— *The Face of the Third Reich*. Pantheon, 1970.

Fleischner, Eva (ed.). *Auschwitz: Beginning of a New Era?* KTAV, 1977.

———— *Judaism in German Christian Theology Since 1945*. Scarecrow, 1975.

Flender, Harold. *Rescue in Denmark*. Simon and Schuster, 1963.

Frank, Anne. *The Diary of a Young Girl*. Pocket Books, 1965.

Frankl, Viktor. *Man's Search for Meaning*. (Original title: *From Death-Camp To Existentialism*, 1959.) Beacon, 1963.

Friedlander, Albert H., (ed.). *Out of the Whirlwind*. Schocken, 1976.

Friedlander, Saul. *Kurt Gerstein: The Ambiguity of Good.*

Knopf, 1969.

_____ *Pius XII and the Third Reich: A Documentation.* Knopf, 1966.

Friedman, Phillip. *Martyrs and Fighters.* Praeger, 1954.

_____ *Their Brothers' Keepers.* Crown, 1957.

Friedman, Saul S. *No Haven for the Oppressed.* Wayne State University Press, 1973.

Garlinski, Josef. *Fighting Auschwitz.* Fawcett, 1976.

Gershan, Karen. *Selected Poems.* Harcourt, Brace and World, 1966.

Gilbert, G.M. *Nuremberg Diary.* Farrar, Straus, and Giroux, 1947.

Gilbert, Martin. *The Holocaust.* Hill and Wang, 1979.

Glatstein, Jacob, Israel Knox and Samuel Margoshes, (eds.). *Anthology of Holocaust Literature.* The Jewish Publication Society of America, 1969.

Glock, Charles, Gertrude Selznick, and Joe Spaeth. *The Apathetic Majority.* Harper and Row, 1966.

Goebbels, Joseph. *Final Entries 1945.* Putnam, 1978.

_____ *The Goebbels Diaries.* Greenwood (reprint of 1948 edition).

Goldstein, Bernard. *The Stars Bear Witness.* Viking, 1949.

Goldstein, Charles, *The Bunker.* The Jewish Publication Society of America, 1970.

Gollwitzer, Helmut, Kathe Kuhn, Reinhold Schneider, (eds.). *Dying We Live.* Pantheon, 1956.

Gordon, Harold J., Jr. *Hitler and the Beer Hall Putsch.* Princeton University Press, 1972.

Green, Gerald. *The Artists of Terezin.* Hawthorn, 1969.

Grossman, Mendel. *With A Camera In The Ghetto.* Schocken, 1977.

Habe, Hans. *The Mission.* Coward-McCann, 1966.

Halperin, Irving. *Messengers from the Dead.* Westminster, 1970.

Harris, Whitney R. *Tyranny on Trial.* Southern Methodist University Press, 1954.

Hausner, Gideon. *Justice In Jerusalem.* Harper and Row, 1966.

Hay, Malcolm. *Thy Brother's Blood.* Hart, 1975.

Heartfield, John. *Photomontages of the Nazi Period.* Universe, 1977.

Heiden, Konrad. *Der Fuehrer: Hitler's Rise to Power.* Beacon, 1969.

Heimler, Eugene. *Concentration Camp.* (Original Title: *Night of the Mist,* 1959.) Pyramid Books, 1961.

Hermanns, William. *Holocaust.* Harper and Row, 1972.

Hersey, John. *The Wall.* Knopf, 1950.

Hersh, Gizelle and Peggy Mann. *Gizelle, Save the Children.* Everest, 1980.

Herzstein, Edwin. *Adolph Hitler and The German Trauma, 1913-1945.* Putnam, 1974.

Hilberg, Raul. *The Destruction of the European Jews.* Quadrangle, 1961.

———— (ed.). *Documents of Destruction.* Quadrangle, 1971.

————, et al, (eds.). *The Warsaw Diary of Adam Czerniakow.* Stein and Day, 1979.

Hillel, Marc and Clarissa Henry. *Of Pure Blood.* McGraw-Hill, 1977.

Hilsenrath, Edgar. *The Nazi and the Barber.* Doubleday, 1971.

Hitler, Adolph. *Mein Kampf.* Houghton Mifflin, 1943.

Hochhuth, Rolf. *The Deputy.* Grove Press, 1964.

Hoess, Rudolf. *Commandant of Auschwitz.* World, 1960.

Hohne, Heinz. *The Order of the Death's Head.* Coward-

McCann, 1970.

Horbach, Michael. *Out of the Night.* Frederick Fell, 1967.

Hull, David Stewart. *Film in the Third Reich.* Simon and Schuster, 1973.

Hyams, Joseph. *A Field of Buttercups.* Prentice-Hall, 1968.

_____ *I Never Saw Another Butterfly.* McGraw-Hill, 1964.

Iranek-Osmecki, Kazimierz. *He Who Saves One Life.* Crown, 1971.

Irving, David. *Hitler's War.* Viking, 1977.

Isaac, Jules. *The Teaching of Contempt.* Holt, Rinehart and Winston, 1964.

Jackel, Eberhard. *Hitler's Weltanschauung.* Wesleyan University Press, 1972.

Jacot, Michael. *The Last Butterfly.* Bobbs-Merrill, 1974.

Jarman. T.L., *The Rise and Fall of Nazi Germany.* New York University Press, 1956.

Jaspers, Karl. *The Question of German Guilt.* Dial, 1947.

Jewish Black Book Committee. *The Black Book, The Nazi Crime Against the Jewish People.* Duell, Sloan and Pearce, 1946.

Kalow, Gert. *The Shadow of Hitler.* Quadrangle, 1971.

Kantor, Alfred. *The Book of Alfred Kantor.* McGraw-Hill, 1971.

Kaplan, Chaim A. *The Scroll of Agony.* (Reprinted as *The Warsaw Diary of Chaim Kaplan.*) Macmillan, 1965.

Karmel, Ilona. *An Estate of Memory.* Houghton Mifflin, 1969.

Karmel-Wolfe, Henia. *The Baders of Jacob Street.* Lippincott, 1970.

Katz, Alfred. *Poland's Ghettos at War.* Twayne, 1970.

Katz, Robert. *Black Sabbath.* Macmillan, 1969.

Ka-tzetnik. *Atrocity.* Lyle Stuart, 1963.

———— *House of Dolls.* Pyramid, 1960.

Kessel, Sim. *Hanged at Auschwitz.* Stein and Day, 1972.

Klarsfield, Beate. *Wherever They May Be.* Vanguard, 1974.

Klein, Gerda. *All But My Life.* Hill and Wang, 1957.

Koestler, Arthur. *Scum of the Earth.* Macmillan, 1968.

Kogon, Eugen. *The Theory and Practice of Hell.* Farrar, Straus and Cudihy, 1950.

Kohn, Nahum and Howard Roiter. *A Voice from the Forest.* Schocken, 1980.

Korczak, Janusz. *Ghetto Diary.* Schocken, 1978.

Korman, Gerd, (ed.). *Hunter and Hunted: Human History of the Holocaust.* Viking, 1973.

Kosinski, J. *The Painted Bird.* Pocket Books, 1966.

Kuper, Jack. *Child of the Holocaust.* Doubleday, 1968.

Kurzman, Dan. *The Bravest Battle.* Putnam, 1976.

Kuznetsov, Anatoly. *Babi Yar.* Farrar, Straus and Giroux, 1970.

Langer, Lawrence L. *The Holocaust and the Literary Imagination.* Yale University Press, 1975.

Langfus, Anna. *The Whole Land Brimstone.* Pantheon, 1962.

Leboucher, Fernande. *Incredible Mission.* Doubleday, 1969.

Leiser, Erwin. *Nazi Cinema.* Macmillan, 1975.

Leitner, Isabella. *Fragments of Isabella.* Crowell, 1978.

Levi, Primo. *If This Man Is a Man.* Orion, 1959. (Later published as *Survival in Auschwitz.*)

Levin, Meyer. *Eva.* Simon and Schuster, 1959.

Levy, Claud and Paul Tillard. *Betrayal at the Vel d'Hviv.* Hill and Wang, 1969.

Lewinska, Pelagia. *Twenty Months at Auschwitz.* Lyle Stuart, 1968.

Lewy, Gunter. *The Catholic Church and Nazi Germany.*

McGraw-Hill, 1964.

Lind, Jakov. *Landscape in Concrete*. Grove, 1966.

———— *Soul of Wood and Other Stories*. Fawcett, 1966.

Littell, Franklin H. *The Crucifixion of the Jews*. Harper and Row, 1975.

———— *The German Church Struggle and the Holocaust*. Wayne State University Press, 1974.

———— *The German Phoenix*. Doubleday, 1960.

Lustig, Arnost. *Darkness Casts No Shadow*. Inscape, 1976.

———— *Diamonds of the Night*. Inscape, 1978.

———— *Night and Hope*. Inscape, 1976.

———— *A Prayer for Katerina Horovitzova*. Harper and Row, 1973.

Maile, Florence and Michael Selzer. *The Nuremberg Mind*. Quadrangle, 1975.

Mann, Peggy and Ruth Kluger. *The Last Escape*. Doubleday, 1973.

Manvell, Roger and Heinrich Fraenkel. *Dr. Goebbels: His Life and Death*. Simon and Schuster, 1960.

———— *The Incomparable Crime*. Putnam, 1967.

Manvell, Roger. *S.S. And Gestapo*. Ballantine, 1969.

Mark, Ber. *Uprising in the Warsaw Ghetto*. Schocken, 1975.

Maser, Werner, (ed.). *Hitler's Letters and Notes*. Harper and Row, 1974.

Masters, Anthony. *The Summer That Bled*. St. Martin's, 1972.

Maurel, Michelene. *An Ordinary Camp*. Simon and Schuster, 1958.

McGarry, Michael B. *Christology After Auschwitz*. Paulist, 1977.

Meinecke, Fredrich. *The German Catastrophe*. Peter Smith, 1963.

Merkl, Peter H. *The Making of a Stormtrooper.* Princeton University, 1980.

Michel, Jean. *Dora.* Holt Rinehart Winston, 1980.

Minco, Marga. *Bitter Herbs.* Oxford University Press, 1960.

Mitscherlich, Alexander and Margareta. *The Inability to Mourn.* Grove, 1975.

Mitscherlich, Alexander and Fred Mielke. *Doctors of Infamy.* H. Schuman, 1960.

Moose, George, (ed.). *Nazi Culture.* Grosset and Dunlap, 1968.

Morley, John F. *Vatican Diplomacy and the Jews During the Holocaust, 1939-1943.* KTAV, 1980.

Morse, Arthur D. *While Six Million Died.* Random House, 1967.

Mosley, Leonard. *The Reich Marshall.* Dell, 1975.

Muller, Filip. *Eyewitness Auschwitz.* Stein and Day, 1979.

Napora, Paul. *Auschwitz.* Naylor, 1967.

———— *Death at Belsen.* Naylor, 1967.

Naumann, Bernd. *Auschwitz.* Praeger, 1966.

Naumann, Peter. *Black March.* William Sloan, 1958.

Newman, Judith Sternberg. *In the Hell of Auschwitz.* Exposition, 1963.

Newmann, Robert. *The Pictorial History of the Third Reich.* Bantam, 1962.

Noakes, Jeremy and Geoffrey Pridham (eds.). *Documents on Nazism, 1919-1945.* Viking, 1975.

Novitch, Miriam. *Sobibor.* Schocken, 1980.

Nyiszli, Miklos. *Auschwitz.* Frederick Fell, 1960.

Orlow, Dietrich. *A History of the Nazi Party, 1919-1933.* University of Pittsburgh Press, 1969.

Papanak, Ernst, with Edward Linn. *Out of the Fire.* Morrow,

1975.

Pawelezynska, Anna. *Values and Violence in Auschwitz.* University of California, 1979.

Pearlman, Moshe. *The Capture and Trial of Adolf Eichmann.* Simon and Schuster, 1963.

Perl, Gisella. *I Was A Doctor in Auschwitz.* International Universities Press, 1948.

Pilch, Judah, (ed.). *The Jewish Catastrophe in Europe.* American Association for Jewish Education, 1968.

Pinkus, Oscar. *The House of Ashes.* World, 1964.

Poliakov, Leon. *Harvest of Hate.* Syracuse University Press, 1954.

Prager, Moshe. *Sparks of Glory.* Shengold, 1974.

Presser, Jacob. *The Destruction of the Dutch Jews.* Dutton, 1969.

Rabinowitz, Dorothy. *New Lives.* Knopf. 1976.

Rawicz, Piotr. *Blood from the Sky.* Harcourt, Brace and World, 1964.

Reitlinger, Gerold. *The Final Solution.* Beechhurst, 1953.

_____ *The SS: Alibi of a Nation, 1922-1945.* Viking, 1957.

Remak, Joachim, (ed.). *The Nazi Years.* Prentice-Hall, 1969.

Ringelblum, Emmanuel. *Notes from the Warsaw Ghetto.* McGraw-Hill, 1958.

_____ *Polish-Jewish Relations During the Second World War.* Howard Fertig, 1976.

Robertson, Esmonde M. *Hitler's Pre-War Policy and Military Plans 1933-1939.* Citadel, 1967.

Robinson, Jacob. *And the Crooked Shall Be Made Straight.* Macmillan, 1965.

Robinson, Jacob, and Yehuda Bauer, (eds.). *Guide to Unpublished Materials of the Holocaust Period.* Jerusalem, "Ahva" Cooperative Press, vol. I 1970, vol. II 1972, vol.

III 1975.

Roper, Edith and Clara Leiser. *Nazi Justice*. Dutton, 1941.

Rosen, Donia. *The Forest, My Friend*. World Federation of Bergen-Belsen Associations, 1971.

Rosenbaum, Irving. *The Holocaust and Halakhah*. KTAV, 1976.

Roskies, David, (ed.). *Night Words: A Midrash on the Holocaust*. B'nai B'rith Hillel Foundations, 1971.

Rousset, David. *The Other Kingdom*. Reynal and Hitchcock, 1947.

Rubenstein, Richard L. *After Auschwitz*. Bobbs-Merrill, 1966.

Ruether, Rosemary R. *Faith and Fratricide*. Seabury, 1974.

Russell, Lord of Liverpool. *The Scourge of the Swastika*. Ballantine, 1956.

Rutherford, Ward. *Genocide*. Ballantine, 1973.

Sachs, Nelly. *O The Chimneys*. Farrar, Straus and Giroux, 1967.

Salomon, Charlotte. *Charlotte: A Diary in Pictures*. Harcourt Brace, 1963.

Samuel, Maurice. *The Great Hatred*. Knopf, 1948.

Schaeffer, Susan Fromberg. *Anya*. Macmillan, 1974.

Schleunes, Karl A. *The Twisted Road to Auschwitz*. University of Illinois Press, 1970.

Schoenberner, Gerhard. *The Yellow Star*. Bantam, 1973.

Schuman, Frederick Lewis. *The Nazi Dictatorship*. Knopf, 1936.

Schwarz-Bart, Andre. *The Last of the Just*. Bantam, 1960.

Selzer, Michael. *The Last Hours at Dachau*. Lippincott, 1978.

Semprun, Jorge. *The Long Voyage*. Grove, 1964.

Senesh, Hannah. *Hannah Senesh—Her Life and Diary*. Schocken, 1972.

Sereny, Gitta. *Into That Darkness.* McGraw-Hill, 1974.

Shapell, Natham. *Witness to the Truth.* McKay, 1974.

Shirer, William L. *The Rise and Fall of the Third Reich.* Simon and Schuster, 1960.

Shub, Borid, (ed.). *Hitler's Ten Year War on the Jews.* Institute of Jewish Affairs, 1943.

Smith, Bradley. *Adolph Hitler.* Hoover Institution Press, 1967.

_____ *Heinrich Himmler.* Hoover Institute Press, 1971.

_____ *Reaching Judgment at Nuremberg.* Basic Books, 1976.

Smith, Marcus J. *The Harrowing of Hell: Dachau.* University of New Mexico Press, 1972.

Snell, John L., (ed.). *The Nazi Revolution—Germany's Guilt or Germany's Fate?* D.C. Heath, 1959.

Snyder, Louis L. *Encyclopedia of the Third Reich.* McGraw-Hill, 1976.

_____ *Hitler and Nazism.* Bantam, 1971.

Speer, Albert. *Inside the Third Reich.* Macmillan, 1970.

_____ *Spandau.* Macmillan, 1976.

Sperber, Manes. *. . . than a Tear in the Sea.* World Federation of Bergen-Belsen Associations, 1967.

Stein, George. *The Waffen SS.* Cornell University Press, 1970.

Steiner, Jean-Francois. *Treblinka.* Simon and Schuster, 1967.

Stochura, Peter D. *Nazi Youth in the Weimar Republic.* Clio, 1975.

Stroop, Juergen. *The Stroop Report.* Pantheon, 1979.

Suhl, Yuril, (ed.). *They Fought Back.* Schocken, 1967.

Sydnor, Charles W., Jr. *Soldiers of Destruction.* Princeton University, 1977.

Syrkin, Marie. *Blessed Is the Match.* Jewish Publication Society of America, 1947.

Szmaglewska, Seweryna. *Smoke Over Birkenau.* Holt, 1947.

Taylor, Telford. *Sword and Swastika.* Simon and Schuster, 1952.

Thalman, Rita and Feinermann, Emmanuel. *Crystal Night.* Coward, McCann and Geoghegan, 1974.

Thomas, Gordon and Max Morgan Witts. *Voyages of the Damned.* Fawcett, 1975.

Toland, John. *Adolf Hitler.* Doubleday, 1976.

Toll, Nelly. *Without Surrender.* Running Press, 1978.

Tomkiewicz, Mina. *Of Bombs and Mice.* A.S. Barnes, 1970.

Trevor-Roper, H.R. *The Last Days of Hitler.* Macmillan, 1947.

Trunk, Isaiah. *Jewish Reponses to Nazi Persecutors.* Stein and Day, 1979.

———— *Judenrat.* Macmillan, 1972.

Tushnet, Leonard. *The Pavement of Hell.* St. Martin's, 1972.

———— *To Die with Honor.* Citadel, 1965.

Viereck, Peter. *Metapolitics.* Capricorn, 1961.

Waite, Robert G.L. *The Psychopathic God.* Basic Books, 1977.

Wells, Leon W. *The Death Brigade.* Schocken, 1978.

Wheaton, Eliot Barculo. *The Nazi Revolution 1933-1935.* Anchor, 1969.

Wiechert, Ernst. *The Forest of the Dead.* Greenberg, 1947.

Wiesel, Elie. *Night.* Hill and Wang, 1960.

Wiesenthal, Simon. *The Murderers Among Us.* McGraw-Hill, 1967.

Wighton, Charles. *Heydrich: Hitler's Most Evil Henchman.* Chilton, 1962.

Yahil, Leni. *The Rescue of Danish Jewry.* Jewish Publication Society of America, 1969.

Zahn, Gordon C. *German Catholics and Hitler's Wars.* Sheed and Ward, 1962.

_____ *In Solitary Witness.* Irvington, 1964.

Zeiger, Henry A. (ed.). *The Case Against Adolf Eichmann.* New American Library, 1960.

Ziemian, Joseph. *The Cigarette Sellers of Three Crosses Square.* Lerner, 1970.

Zuckerman, Isaac, (ed.). *The Fighting Ghettos.* Belmont-Tower, 1971.

Zylberberg, Michael. *A Warsaw Diary.* Hartmore, 1969.